D1453816

St. Paul's Within the Walls
Rome

A HISTORY AND GUIDE, 1870–1980

JUDITH RICE MILLON

ST. PAUL'S WITHIN THE WALLS

Watercolor perspective and ground plan of St. Paul's Within the Walls, signed George Edmund Street, 1875. The tympanum mosaic, the ironwork of the churchyard railing and the building of the rectory were not to be undertaken for several years. (Photo: Thomas P. Lang, Boston)

St. Paul's Within the Walls Rome

A BUILDING HISTORY AND GUIDE, 1870–1980

Judith Rice Millon

WILLIAM L. BAUHAN, PUBLISHER
DUBLIN, NEW HAMPSHIRE

COPYRIGHT © 1982 BY JUDITH RICE MILLON

All rights reserved. No portion of this book may be reproduced without permission of the publisher, except by reviewers quoting brief passages in newspapers or periodicals.

Library of Congress Cataloguing in Publication Data:

Millon, Judith Rice, 1934–
    St. Paul's within the walls, Rome.
    Bibliography: p.
    Includes index.
    1. St. Paul's Church (Rome, Italy)   I. Title.
NA5620.S98M5   726'.5'0945632   81-8055
ISBN 0-87233-058-3   AACR2

Printed in the United States of America

To Wilbur Charles Woodhams

Rector of St. Paul's Within the Walls, 1961–1981

Man of spirit and a friend

Contents

List of Illustrations

COLOR PLATES FOLLOWING PAGE 75

Foreword

Recently I looked east from the private library where John Paul II was graciously receiving in audience Rome's Anglican clergy and their wives, and I could make out the spire of St. Paul's Within the Walls. In that same room John XXIII had told me how as a student he had walked past St. Paul's each day, enjoyed the ringing of the bells, and was sorry he could not enter. Built during the first years of a liberated and unified Italy, St. Paul's was to be a reminder to Rome that the Pauline tradition compliments the Petrine in the catholicity of the Church.

The words spoken at the dedication of St. Paul's in 1876 made that reminder in a profound concern for the unity of the church and for the plain speaking in love that eventually opens hearts and minds. There is a perception of the meaning of the Reformation and of catholicity in the building of St. Paul's which has taken a hundred years to come into consciousness. In the following account of the building of St. Paul's you will recognize that each generation has made the building a growing, living thing. Our church has never been a museum or simply a great work of art and architecture. The few minor changes and additions in these past twenty years have been mostly related to worship—to keep the building alive in its function without changing the architect's basic concepts. Changes involving the altar and *schola cantorum* were envisioned years earlier by Walter Lowrie. The Great Doors were a spontaneous response to the opening towards unity in the time of John XXIII and a constant reminder of one of the reasons for our presence in Rome.

Robert Nevin began his thirty-seven years' ministry at St. Paul's with a mission to make the Church of Rome aware that the Church's true nature includes St. Paul as well as St. Peter. When his successor, Walter Lowrie, began his twenty-three years as rector the parish had a different feel to it: it was established, institutionalized, and still American. When I began my twenty years' ministry in Rome in 1961 it was to a thriving, solidly American, pan-Protestant community enjoying the full amenities of post-war Roman life. But these twenty years have been a microcosm of the world's changes. Today St. Paul's congregation consists not only of American Anglicans but of Christians from every part of the world. Our vision of ourselves and of our ministry has changed, our corporate sense is less provincial and our buildings teem with life that other generations could not have imagined. Being less homogeneous racially, politically, educationally and economically than before, we have come to find at St. Paul's that our oneness truly is in Christ and needs always to be sought after. Where we once had seen ourselves as missionaries, today we find our lives enriched by sharing a ministry with Christians whose backgrounds and presuppositions ask questions of ours.

Any building is a monument and a message to later times. Judith Rice Millon's appreciation and history of the building helps us to cherish both the ideals that brought it all about, and their expression. Friends and admirers of St. Paul's will always be grateful for this and for her careful scholarship and documentation. I am thankful for twenty years of worship, work, and living with the great work of architecture and art which is St. Paul's Within the Walls, and also thankful that it has been sometimes in the companionship of Judy and Henry Millon, who helped me to see its beauty.

WILBUR CHARLES WOODHAMS
St. Paul's Within the Walls, Rome, Italy
Feast of the Conversion of St. Paul, 1981

12

Introduction

THE TWO RECTORS who built St. Paul's Within the Walls, Robert Jenkins Nevin and his successor Walter Lowrie, each published an account of the construction and decoration of the church carried out under their supervision. The two journals are far livelier and more descriptive than the contemporary Vestry notes or building records. They reveal, through the rectors' changing views over a period of some fifty years, the political and religious attitudes that affected Protestant Episcopal thinking in the Eternal City.

Nevin, former Union artillery officer in the Civil War, brought to Rome the stalwart resolve of the soldier, American convictions of liberty and equality, and an unswerving hostility to the Papacy. His mission was to return St. Paul, the guiding apostle of the Protestants since the Reformation, to his original position beside Peter as joint protector and founder of Christ's church. Lowrie, who could be as outspoken as Nevin, fortunately brought to his ministry an eloquence tempered by toleration of, and even reconciliation with, the Roman Church.

Standing today on attitudes of ecumenical belief and action, but heirs of such recent history, we may be interested in, embarrassed for, or amused by some of these earlier attitudes. The ideas from which they sprang were, however, wholly serious in their time, and reveal more about the choice of site, form, and decoration of St. Paul's Within the Walls than the factual construction records and building contracts.

In December of 1869, the year Nevin arrived to become rector of what was then called Grace Church, Pius IX convened the First Vatican Council. The following summer, on

18 July 1870, the council promulgated the decree of Papal Infallibility, *Pastor Aeternus*. Nothing could have more inflamed the multitude of Protestant grievances toward papal authority in Rome. But even as the Roman church was on the one hand collecting and intensifying its spiritual focus, it was on the other coming to the dissolution of its temporal power. On 20 September of the same year, the Vatican Army was defeated by troops fighting for the united Kingdom of Italy—and Rome, capital city of the Caesars and the Popes, became capital of a new secular Italian state.

Victor Emmanuel's government opened the gates of Rome to dissident worship—in fact its new constitution protected religious freedom. In his account Dr. Nevin expresses, with all the vigor of his cause, the Anglican jubilation at this "recovery of Italy to the Christian Faith." He reviews the early years of the American Episcopalians in Rome, from the difficulties of their initial assembly in 1859 to the consecration of St. Paul's Within the Walls in 1876. Dr. Lowrie, who succeeded Dr. Nevin in 1907, continues the account of the church through 1926, reflecting not only the color of his own personality but the new spiritual attitudes as they had become modified with the passage of time.

Lowrie, who had trained as a classicist as an undergraduate at Princeton and was a Fellow of the American School of Classical Studies in Rome during 1895–1896, was a Christian archaeologist as well as a theologian. A copious scholar, Lowrie is particularly noted for his work on the Danish philosopher Kierkegaard, and among art historians for *Monuments of the Early Church*. His total bibliography numbers thirty-eight books and fifty-nine major articles. Three publications are of particular interest to this history: *Fifty Years of St. Paul's American Church, Action in the Liturgy,* and *Ss. Peter and Paul in Rome.*

The latter book, published in 1940, had its inception during Lowrie's years as rector of St. Paul's, when an uneasy and somewhat aloof peace characterized the relations between the Roman and Protestant churches. In the text Lowrie looked back to the founding of the early church and to what he called the "great schism" between St. Peter, Apostle to the Jews, and St. Paul, Apostle to the Gentiles. He made an analogy between this early separation and later reconciliation, and his own mission in Rome:

Perhaps in completing St. Paul's Within-the-Walls I might have found some way of asserting in monumental form . . . that it is formality which divides us, the form of church organization, and other things comparatively indifferent, which separate those who hold substantially the same faith, and artificially unite many who in the matter of faith are far apart. (Lowrie, *Peter and Paul*: pp. 118–19)

Dr. Lowrie anticipated the ecumenism rekindled by Pope John XXIII and the Second Vatican Council, a mission that has been central to St. Paul's under the present rector, Wilbur Charles Woodhams.

In addition to the early records of Nevin and Lowrie and the Vestry Minutes, this guide to the church and its building history also depends on art and architectural studies of the Burne-Jones mosaics and of the building itself, a notable example of late Italian Gothic Revival architecture by the eminent British architect George Edmund Street. Richard Dorment's dissertation for Columbia University, *Burne-Jones and the Decoration of St. Paul's American Church, Rome*, has been invaluable, both for Dorment's own observations and for the extensive correspondence on the church decoration that he compiled.

I am indebted to Vestry members and parishioners alike for sharing their interests, concerns, and studies on the history of the church. Architect C. Ronald Ostberg has been a source for information on current preservation and conservation of the building. Sculptor Peter Rockwell and classicist Rogers Scudder have made numerous thoughtful observations, patiently checking building details that I was unable to do from Boston and—with the Acts of the Apostles in hand, a lot of neck-craning, and the bright-eyed help of Mary Rockwell—they have supplied information on the stained glass windows. Captain Brown Taylor, who is preparing a history of the Vestry, kindly shared with me his copies of the Vestry Minutes. My thanks also go to the architectural firm of Brown Daltas and Associates, with offices in Rome and Boston, for acting as courier for correspondence on several occasions.

The rector has been not only the initiator and gentle goad for the overall project, but has acted as a personal guide to the rectory and to the redesigned chancel, now adapted under his supervision to the new liturgy. He and sculptor Carl Stern, custodian of the church, were my guides to the scary heights of the belfry, its bells ready to ring again when restoration funds make possible the strengthening of the tower. My husband, Henry Millon, has generously shared with me his broad scholarship in the field of architectural history as well as his knowledge and familiarity with St. Paul's.

A social history of St. Paul's waits to be written. Out of the multitude of American tourists and residents in Rome, the church has attracted a notable roster of artists, scholars, industrialists and bankers, as well as a liberal salting of rogues and ne'er-do-wells, both male and female. The names of many of the Vestry, Wardens, and benefactors are familiar to those interested in this period of American history. They have been mentioned in this guide, however, only as they have influenced the building or decoration of St. Paul's.

I

A BUILDING HISTORY

A Building History

O N 25 JANUARY 1873, the Feast of the Conversion of St. Paul, the cornerstone of St. Paul's Church in Rome was laid. Among the memorabilia placed under the cornerstone is a brick from Independence Hall in Philadelphia. Its inclusion symbolized the hope, as expressed by the rector, Dr. Robert Nevin, that this new church would be "a constant visible witness . . . that religious liberty and the rights of human conscience have at last found a home in the city of the Popes and the Caesars." Little more than a hundred years later, the change from challenge to reconciliation between the Roman and Anglican churches was given joyous recognition at St. Paul's. On 28 April 1977, the Archbishop of Canterbury, with the President of the Pontifical Secretariat for Christian Unity, dedicated great bronze entrance doors to the church. Conceived as a tribute to the *aggiornamento* of Pope John XXIII and a new age of Christian unity, the sculptured doors on one of Rome's busiest streets, bear daily witness to the healing progress of ecumenism.

Robert Jenkins Nevin (rect. 1869–1906) came to Rome in time to observe the last months of the temporal authority of the Papacy. The Kingdom of Italy was preparing to claim Rome for its own capital. The papal army, diminished by the transfer of troops to the Franco-Prussian War, was too weak to turn back the siege of King Victor Emmanuel II's vigorous Italians. On 20 September 1870, the Roman wall was breached near the Porta Pia. Italian troops poured through the opening, and the Pope's political power over the Eternal City was ended.

With the new order came a new constitution protecting freedom of worship. The Protestant congregations in Rome had longed for this moment. The Papacy had tolerated dissident religious services *within* the walls of Rome only when such services were protected by the roof of a diplomatic legation; without such protection papal order unequivocally banished the foreign chapels to *without* the walls. Relations between Pontifical and Protestant churches, while frequently resolved in personal friendships and social interchange, were nonetheless strained and often bitter. Dr. Nevin minced neither words nor attitude in his history of the church, *St. Paul's Within the Walls: An Account of the American Chapel at Rome, Italy*.

A Union artillery major in the Civil War, Nevin combined leadership and tenacity with a sure aesthetic sense. He was the principal builder of the church, and though Vestry members over the years included many practicing artists as well as heirs to American fortunes, Nevin was both artistic guide and principal fundraiser. A memorial plaque over the sacristy door proclaims Nevin "a soldier for union and freedom" and records that "this temple is his monument."

The roots of the church date to the spring of 1859, when the first celebration of Holy Communion according to the liturgy of the American Episcopal Church was held in the house of sculptor Joseph Mozier. Since the end of the eighteenth century, Americans from the young republic had been venturing in increasing numbers to Rome, sometimes to settle down but more usually as tourists to this great source of classical antiquity and Renaissance art. By the time of our Civil War at least two-hundred Americans were resident in Rome; hotel registers, consular notes, and newspaper clippings recorded thousands more visitors annually. A visit to this wellhead of civilization—and one of the great Christian sites, even for Protestants—was a compelling travel vogue.

The Sunday gathering of Episcopalians at Joseph Mozier's house did not pass unnoticed by the papal government; a "significant and warning remark" stated clearly that such worship had to find shelter under the seal of the American Legation. Thus began a period of nine years in which the place of Sunday worship changed continuously according to availability of "legation chapels." When the United States Congress withdrew financial support of the legation in 1867, effectively closing it down, it became evident that Grace Church, as the parish was then called, would have to find a meeting place outside the Roman walls. Following an example set by the English, the American congregation rented a former granary just outside the Porta del Popolo, a gate guarded for several centuries by a harmonious pair of Baroque statues of Saints Peter and Paul. The chapel was almost certainly part of the *gabelliere,* or toll collector's station, that stood on the west corner across from the *porta.* Today the expanded piazza and the rushing traffic seem to deny that such a building ever existed.

The environs of the new space were not wholly congenial: on weekdays the vendibles of the open hog market grunted in the neighboring street; yet the chapel was adjacent not only to the English place of worship but to the entrance to the fashionable Borghese Gardens. According to Nevin

the situation was inconvenient, and the neighborhood very objectionable; but inside it was comfortable, and even attractive. There were, however, two serious objections to it: one, the very trying stairway, an inclined plane, up which in former days mules carried their loads of corn and wheat; the other the lowness of the ceiling, which was not sufficient for a perfect ventilation when the chapel was full . . . the room was large, with over five–hundred sittings . . . (Nevin: p. 24)

It was fortunately the practice of the church to close during the summer months, until the Americans struck an arrangement with the English of staying open on alternate summers. Given the Victorian fondness for long sermons and whalebone, a yearning for Gothic heights must have waxed from Sunday to Sunday from May to September. Nevertheless, this chapel served the congregation until the new church was opened in 1876.

The Move to Via Nazionale

Only six years elapsed between the decision to move inside the walls until the consecration of St. Paul's. This is remarkable since there were several international obstacles to overcome: a great part of the money had to be raised from distant benefactors in the United States; the architect was English, and the plans and specifications, prepared according to British practice, had to be interpreted according to Roman building practice; and the Italian and French workmen had never seen, let alone constructed, many of the architectural forms that were required for the new church.

Just twelve days after the defeat of the papal forces, Nevin and the Vestry had resolved to move "within the city gates at the earliest day practicable." By spring of 1871 the American Episcopal Authority in New York had approved this first resolution, but, even more important, they had granted permission not simply to rent or convert an existing building but to build a church that would express religious freedom and American democracy within the walls of Rome.

Nevin sailed to New York that summer on the first of seven arduous transatlantic fundraising trips. These six years, as he was to write, were full of heavy and unbroken toil and anxiety, a period when, in addition to his demanding duties as rector, he served as full-time building supervisor and principal fundraiser.

Nevin spent the late fall and winter of 1871 back in Rome, considering possible building sites and the even more essential "future tenure and constitution" of the church. Towards the end of the year the Vestry decided to change the name from Grace Church to St. Paul's Church. Vestry notes of 1871 record that "the present name of our congregation, Grace Church, cannot be rendered in Italian with any proper significance." Nevin clarified this generality with the abrupt explanation that "'grace' in a Roman mind is hopelessly associated with the Madonna, and had we attempted to carry over the original name . . . it would have stood to the popular mind as the church of the 'Madonna delle Grazie'." (Nevin: p. 53)

The following spring an act of the legislature of the State of New York created a church board with the title "Trustees of St. Paul's American Protestant Episcopal Church, Rome." It was determined that the board would hold title to the property, while the Vestry in Rome would oversee "the immediate management and control of St. Paul's Church, and the maintenance of the church edifice and other property thereof." It was further agreed that the consent of the board would be necessary to confirm the election of a rector.

It is more than likely that Nevin had the controlling voice in the dedication of the church. In his notes he remarks that "by a singularly significant omission" there was no Roman church dedicated to St. Paul inside the city, only the great basilica off the via Ostiense, known throughout the ages as St. Paul's Outside the Walls and believed to be built over the Apostle's tomb. Nevin probably chose to overlook San Paolo (Paolino) alla Regola, just behind the present Ministero di Grazia e Giustizia, by one tradition erected over the house where St. Paul lived. Nevin himself favored the idea that St. Paul had not only lived but preached just around the corner from *his* new church:

The name St. Paul's has been most happy. Nearby is the house of Pudens [now the Church of Santa Pudenziana on via Urbana, between St. Paul's and Santa Maria Maggiore] where the apostle undoubtedly preached. His martyrdom at Rome no one ever has questioned. He was the great Apostle to the Gentiles whose children we are. In his writings, above all others of the sacred books, do we find most clearly set forth the great principles of faith, and liberty, and a pure conscience . . . (Nevin: pp. 53–54)

Building activity at this time was not confined to the Episcopalians. Rome in the last third of the century was preparing for significant changes and expansions. Via Nazionale, until then an area of vineyards and orchards, was planned as the first new street of modern Rome. While it still had a remote, even rural aspect in 1870, it was clearly reserved for an important future as a center of commerce and fashion linking Piazza Venezia, Piazza della Republica, and the nearby Stazione Termini.

For 89,100 Italian lire, or $17,800, the church purchased a 101-foot lot fronting on via Nazionale, with a depth of 182 feet along the east side of via Napoli. The seller was an Italian deputy named Calvo, who had purchased the site a few years earlier from the notorious land speculator, Monsignor de Merode, papal Secretary of War. De Merode in turn had bought it from the Barberini nuns who for centuries had used the land as vineyards. Nevin notes that the value of the land rose 1500 percent between sale by the nuns and purchase by St. Paul's.

Nevin was particular—perhaps so as not to offend the genus loci—that the funds to buy the site should come from Americans in Rome, and his modest initial request for money was readily subscribed by residents and tourists. One of the most interesting of the early gifts was a collection of nineteen paintings and sculptures, donated by American artists working in Rome, among them works by George Inness, Elihu Vedder and John O'Brien Inman. Nevin reported on the

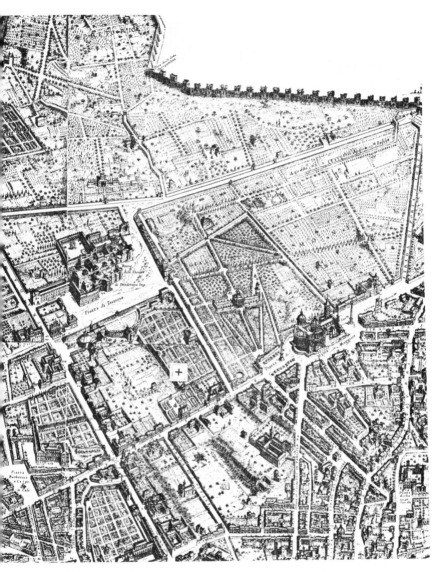

G. B. Falda map, dated 1676, shows the area between the Baths of Diocletian and Santa Maria Maggiore before its development in the last half of the 19th century. The divisions of the orchards and vineyards of the Barberini nuns, where St. Paul's now stands, are clearly marked. (Photo: Thomas P. Lang, Boston)

disposition of these works of art in the summary of his summer's fundraising in the United States, copied into the Vestry Minutes of 28 December 1871. All the works were transported to New York and from there to Baltimore, where they were first exhibited at the General Convention of the Episcopal Church. It was hoped that their sale at auction would net $6,000, but an unforeseen happening suddenly turned charitable monies in another direction:

. . . just at that moment occurred the burning of Chicago—this made their public sale at that time unwise. They were then brought to N.Y. and placed on exhibition and sale at the National Academy of Design.

Church records are obscure about the eventual sale of the pieces in the collection, but certainly the return to the building fund was disappointing. (Today the sale value of an Inness painting alone would not only have purchased the site but made a substantial dent in the construction costs!) A list of these artists, with the titles of their works, is given in the Appendix.

George Edmund Street
and the Building of the Church

"We intend to build a stone church," Nevin wrote to the Friends of the American Chapel in Rome in a fundraising letter of 1871, "distinctively Gothic in Style, to seat not less than 700 . . ." The notes of a meeting held in the rector's rooms on 8 March 1872 indicate that the Vestry was considering at least three architects: "Designs for the new church by Mr. G. E. Street, and Mr. Thos. J. Smith of London and Mr. Luigi Eynard of Rome, were exhibited." However, given Street's outstanding reputation as one of England's foremost architects, inclusion of the other schemes—by architects who are today unknown—may have been a formality.

George Edmund Street (1824–1881), at this time working on designs for the Great Law Courts in London, was a foremost exponent of the Italian Gothic Revival style, and a pillar of the Ecclesiological Movement which drew inspiration from fourteenth-century church rites and building styles. Street had an international reputation and was known to be a swift and prodigious worker. According to his son and biographer, Arthur E. Street (1855–1938), George Edmund Street designed some 260 churches and secular buildings, including the English churches in Rome, Paris, Geneva, and Constantinople, and planned restorations and additions for some 460 others. St. Paul's, which reflects his admiration for North Italian brick and marble and pays particular tribute to San Zeno in Verona, is counted among his finest churches. Seven drawings by Street for the church are preserved in the collection of the Royal Institute of British Architects in London.

In a letter of 25 February 1872, Street wrote to art critic F. G. Stephens:

We are going to start for Rome tomorrow night. I am going to look at a church I have just built for the English at Geneva, and then to look at sites for two churches in Rome—one for the English, the other for the Yankee Episcopalians. By very odd coincidence they both came to me without knowing the other's intentions. (Dorment, *Decoration*: p. 3)

The English hired Street as well, but he began this work after that on St. Paul's. Unfortunately the English church did not progress easily, and after Street's death his plans were substantially modified by Arthur, architect as well as biographer, who took over for his father.

The St. Paul's Vestry Minutes of 12 March, some two weeks after Street had departed from London, name him as architect:

On Motion the design for the New Church of Mr. G. E. Street of London, was adopted, subject to modifications that may be subsequently determined on. This plan, with front of 64′ by depth of 132′, 70′ in height, to seat about 800 persons, and including campanile, Mr. Street declares that he can build for $60,000.

In fact the dimensions changed little, but as is often the way in such matters, the cost more than doubled.

Between 1872 and 1876, Street visited Rome three times according to Nevin, four times according to the biography (which mentions two further visits to Rome before his death in 1881). The longest of the working visits before the consecration was probably only ten days. One of the visits was also a wedding trip with his second wife, perhaps timed to coincide with the original date of 25 January 1876 set by Nevin for the consecration. Unfortunately construction delays postponed the consecration service by two months, and for Street the trip ended in tragedy. Mrs. Street contracted what we may suppose was the treacherous malarial infection called Roman fever. Arthur Street wrote briefly, "they stopped a few fatal days in Rome, and then came rapidly home. Rome was responsible for one more victim." (Street, A. E.: p. 230) It was a cruel personal event in Street's Roman story, particularly in view of his love of Italy and the high level of his professional and personal contributions to St. Paul's (he returned to the church a generous part of his architectural fee).

Ground for the church was broken on 5 November 1872. The excavations reached depths ranging from thirty to fifty-one feet before touching virgin clay on which to set the foundations. Forty feet below where the apse now stands excavators found well-preserved fire-blackened walls as well as copper coins from the reign of Nero. The time and expense of establishing foundation walls were far greater than expected, and at the apse end of the church the depth of the foundation is actually greater than the height of the visible walls above.

Rodolfo Lanciani, who would become one of Italy's greatest archaeologists, supervised construction of the foundation walls and, according to a letter from Nevin of 8 January 1873, in the early stages of the building acted in all ways as "representing the architect [Mr. Street]." The construction of the walls above foundation was under the supervision of Henri Kleffler, a Swiss architect residing in Rome, best remembered there for his design of the Villa Savoia outside the Porta Pia. Kleffler also looked after the accounts of the contractor. It was principally Nevin, however, who controlled the overall program and checked the smallest details. The Street plans were, naturally, detailed for English builders, and thus required not only a first interpretation at the hands of the St. Paul's building committee, but constant rechecking to see that construction corresponded to Street's intent.

Nevin's most tedious chore was to establish accurate cost estimates according to the fixed Roman schedule of prices, which established costs for each minutia of building. Alas, many specifications of the English architect did not even appear on the Roman list, which during the nineteenth century had become better adapted to building modifications than to fresh construction. According to Nevin, Roman builders at this time had "acquired a morbid love for imitation . . . or for making something . . . different from what it is." The prevailing artistic goal was to coax cement to resemble brickwork, or brickwork to resemble a stone wall, etc. To establish English or American standards of structural integrity "required great vigilance." In the end, however, "the workmen had, I think, thoroughly acquired the sense of reality as an essential element in good architecture, and became very proud of this feature in the building." (Nevin: p. 78) The elaborate construction accounts eventually totaled more than twelve hundred sheets of foolscap.

Despite the difficulties, Nevin drew cheer from the fact that by his reckoning costs would be kept to $100,000, a figure that "was considered low, even by Roman architects." Later calculations by Dr. Lowrie indicated that, even without decoration but including the cost of the site, the figure was more nearly $146,000—a substantial rise from the architect's original estimate of $60,000. (Lowrie, *Fifty Years*: p. 52)

In plan, St. Paul's is a longitudinal church with nave, clerestory, and side aisles of seven bays, with an elevated choir and apsidal chancel. The side aisles are vaulted with limestone ribs and brick webs or severies, and the nave spanned by broad trusses with simulated segmental barrel vaults of wood. The transverse masonry arches that span the nave at the entrance to the choir and chancel were used as fields for two of the mosaics by Edward Burne-Jones. On the south the first bay of the side aisle, under the campanile or bell tower, houses the baptistry; the seventh or last bay is walled in to provide a sacristy.

The interior and exterior masonry is composed of what Dr. Nevin called "lake-colored" brick from Siena, alternating in uneven courses with travertine from Tivoli. When the exterior was cleaned with high-pressure water in 1979, the brick was revealed to be indeed colored—probably stained after firing to give it a more pleasing tone.

The facade, drawn from north Italian medieval examples, is simple in outline but bold in detail with the campanile placed asymmetrically to the south. Street's original plan called for the bell tower not only to be attached to the front of the church, but to project a foot and a half forward, thereby strongly accentuating its vertical presence. The concept of an interrupted facade on the new boulevard was, however, flatly rejected by the Roman municipal commission, and the front as it now stands is in one plane. The separateness of the campanile is clearly stated only above the clerestory level.

The double-arched entrance portal, with a mosaic in the pediment, faces via Nazionale. Mosaics of the four Evangelists fill the corners of the west window above. Street's original oak doors with handsome wrought iron scrolls designed by him are now displayed inside the church. The cast bronze doors by sculptor Dimitri Hadzi, were hung in 1977.

The interior masonry of St. Paul's is rich and varied, executed by workmen brought from Marseilles. The bricks, similar to those on the exterior, are thin, measuring 12″ × 6″ × 2″, rising about six courses to the foot. The alternate bands of calcareous stone, identified by Dr. Nevin as *font-vieille,* are from the quarries of Arles, France. A harder variety of the stone, which he calls *estiallades,* is used for the capitals and where greater carrying strength is required.

In 1977 sculptor Peter Rockwell, who has helped to supplement the identification of marble by Nevin and Lowrie, carved gargoyle figures in the corbels of the vault ribs of the sacristy vestibule. The gargoyles are in the same style as several grotesques he had previously sculpted for the National Cathedral in Washington, D.C. Although the vestibule was not added until the eighteen-eighties, it uses the same French stone as in the main part of the church. In the carving Rockwell found the stone to be exceedingly soft. We may suppose Street chose it not only for its pleasing creamy color when freshly cut, but also for this very softness, which kept the cost of working it to a minimum. On the south side of the Canterbury Chapel, a partially carved molding suggests that an apprentice may have first chiseled the stone to a geometrical approximation of the final design, for completion by a master stone-cutter (who in this instance never showed up).

In the nave the clerestory walls are supported by columns of polished red Sardinian granite surrounded by four smaller shafts of dove-colored Carrara marble. The red marble of the bases, perhaps mistakenly identified by Nevin as coming from Perugia, is of uncertain origin. The bases of the shafts and the base molding or *batti scopa* of the church are of a dark gray *bardiglio* from Carrara.

The mosaic work of the floor, laid in what Nevin calls the "Venetian manner," is undistinguished. The tesserae, or individual tiles of mosaic, lie on a bed of brick and clay designed to alleviate the damp chill of masonry floors. Beneath the supporting vaults was the original heating system of forced hot air through wide channels, modeled after the hypocausts of ancient Rome. Whatever its efficiency in antiquity, the system worked poorly at St. Paul's from the beginning. Both Lowrie's account and the Vestry notes are dotted with references to makeshift measures to repair or supplement the heating. The problem was finally put to rest by Dr. Woodhams in 1969, in collaboration with architect Robert da Silva. A particularly timely and generous gift from Mr. and Mrs. Thomas Tinsley of Baltimore allowed the installation of a new forced hot water system.

The improved heating system produced a fringe benefit of some significance—utilization of the crypt space. The crypt was partially cleaned out in 1962 and several years later, under the direction of da Silva, repaved, rewired, repainted, and the stair relocated to give direct access from the courtyard. "Undercroft," as this area is now called, is used for a variety of public and church functions. In the nineteen-sixties a part of the space was used for art exhibitions, and several theater groups, formed by actors "beached" in Italy's film capital, brought English language theater to Rome. Teatro

A date before 1880 for this lonely, late afternoon view of St. Paul's can be safely given by reason of the temporary wooden fence which was still in place. (Photo: Istituto Centrale per il Catalogo e la Documentazione)

Nella Cripta is still producing plays, using the simplest of bleacher seats and a simpler stage.

At the time of the church's consecration in 1876, the principal adornments already in place were a series of seventeen fine stained glass windows, designed for St. Paul's by the English commercial firm of Clayton and Bell. After Morris and Company they were considered the most important stained glass designers of the nineteenth century, and they often worked with Street.

In the vertical wall of the apse, where the mosaic portraits of *The Earthly Paradise* now look out to the nave, Street originally spaced three slender lancet windows filled with stained glass. When the stained glass was removed and the openings bricked up, probably in the fall of 1907 to make way for the mosaic, the glass was transferred to the south clerestory where, until 1980, it was difficult to see and awkwardly framed by the larger windows.

The thirteen stained glass windows of the side aisles and baptistry, worthy of attention for both their design and their colors, narrate events from the life of St. Paul. The sequence begins to the left of the central entrance, then continues on the north wall and on around in a clockwise direction. In the west window, over the main entrance, Christ the King is seated in the center, surrounded by eight Roman martyrs of the early church.

St. Paul's Within the Walls was consecrated on the Feast of the Annunciation, Saturday, 25 March 1876, with the workmen barely finished sweeping up in the east end as the bishops prepared to process in at the west. "It would have involved almost a moral defeat to have postponed the service," Nevin wrote, recounting the exhausting final spurt of effort to bring the building to readiness. (Nevin: p. 82)

Five bishops and an assembly of other clerics gathered from Africa, Great Britain, Gibraltar, and the United States. The dedication services lasted a full week, with an octave of sermons including one from each of the bishops. Dr. Nevin's volume gives the texts of all eight in their entirety. (Many years later, in his history of St. Paul's, Lowrie calculated dryly that the consecration sermon by the Bishop of Long Island must have lasted a full two hours.) The impressive ecclesiastical pageantry accompanied by exhaustively rehearsed music under the direction of Dr. E. H. Monk of York Minster, England, and the moving consecration service itself, combined to produce a triumphant opening for St. Paul's Within the Walls. A charming description and woodcut reproduction of the ceremony appeared in *L'Illustrazione Italiana* of 16 April 1876.

The completion of the campanile during the following summer brought full height and grandeur to the facade, as well as a housing for the splendid chime of twenty-three bells (a gift of Thomas Messenger of Brooklyn), cast for St. Paul's in the foundry of Severin Van Aerschodt of Louvain, Belgium. The dedication ceremony fell by plan on the Fourth of July, 1876, against a display—and even flaunt—of patriotic flags and bunting. It was another grand occasion for Nevin and his new church to make a Protestant and libertarian statement in the heart of Rome. On the largest of the bells are St. Paul's words *Verbum Dei Non Est Alligatum*—"the word of God is not bound." Below in English is the inscription: *To the Glory of God and in Honor of His Holy Apostle Paul, January 29, year of our Lord 1876 and of the Independence of the United States of America 100.* Phrases from the Lord's Prayer, the Apostles' Creed, and the Gloria are cast onto the other bells.

The Burne-Jones Mosaics
and the Decoration of the Church, 1876–1907

St. Paul's was open by 1876, but implementation of the decorative program was paced to the finding of benefactors. During Dr. Nevin's tenure carving of the French stone proceeded in stages as contributions were received: first the capitals, then the arches, and last of all the string courses under the roof. Among the important benefactors of this period was William H. Herriman, who gave the garden wall and the handsome wrought iron fence with gates, or "church-yard railing" as the drawings call it. Designed by Street for the church in 1875, it was made at a later time in England and then shipped to Rome. (Richardson: p. 122) Writing about the three drawings for the railing, now in the collection of the Royal Institute of British Architects, Peter Howell noted:

Street's ironwork was of a most remarkable originality. . . . we see him following no precedent and producing something almost prophetic of Art Nouveau for the splendid, great Italian basilica which he built as the American Church in Rome. (Howell: pp. 34–35)

The greatest undertaking for the future of the church, however, was the mosaic decoration, which was begun in 1881 after receipt of a gift for this purpose from Junius Spencer Morgan, Connecticut-born banker and father of the financier J. P. Morgan.

The first mention of mosaic decoration appeared in a brief description of St. Paul's, probably written by Street, in *The Architect* of 20 November 1875. It was noted at the time that "the apse is roofed with a brick semi-dome which it is hoped will be covered in time with a mosaic." Within thirty years of Street's death this modest projection of a single mosaic had in fact increased six-fold. Today the east end of the

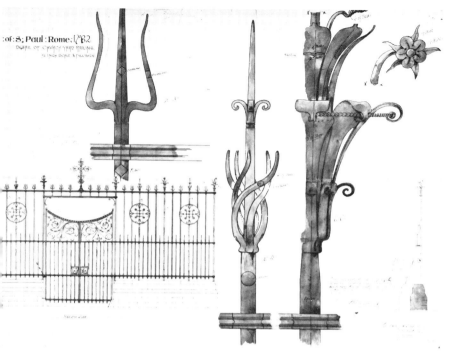

:of: S: Paul : Rome : 1882
DETAIL OF CHURCHYARD RAILING
½ INCH SCALE & FULL SIZE

A detail of the fine churchyard railing, signed in the lower right corner by Street, is in the collection of the Royal Institute of British Architects, London. The text, over the signature of Thomas Potter and Sons, and witnessed by Thomas J. B. Holland, reads: "This is one of the three drawings referred to in the contract signed by us this twenty-eight day of July in the year of our Lord one thousand eight hundred and seventy-nine." (Photo: Courtesy of the Drawings Collection, British Architectural Library, London) church is decorated by the four-part cycle of Edward Burne-Jones's (1833–1898) most ambitious decorative undertaking: in the apse semi-dome is *Christ Enthroned in the Heavenly Jerusalem,* unveiled in 1885; on the two arches of the choir and chancel are *The Annunciation* and *The Tree of Life,* both unveiled in 1894; on the vertical wall of the apse is *The Earthly Paradise,* 1907, which was designed by Burne-Jones but carried out after his death by his former studio assistant, Thomas Matthew Rooke (1842–1942).

On the west wall opposite, a two-part mosaic sequence by George William Breck (1863–1920) was completed in 1913: *The Creation of the World* and *The Adoration of the Magi and Shepherds.* On the exterior, Breck's mosaics also decorate the tympanum over the entrance doors and the frame of the west window.

Six years elapsed between the time of the note in *The Architect* and Street's first verifiable contact with Burne-Jones concerning the design of mosaics for St. Paul's. In his late forties by this time, Burne-Jones was an artistic leader and an outstanding pre-Raphaelite painter—but just why he was chosen for St. Paul's, particularly since he had never before worked in mosaic, is open to surmise. Clayton and Bell might well have been considered, for they had a reputation for their mosaics as well as for their stained glass. As to why no American was proposed, Richard Dorment, a leading scholar of the Burne-Jones mosaics, suggests that while Rome was bursting with expatriate American artists, none of them was appropriate for the task: "in the eighteen-seventies there was no real tradition of American mural decoration. . . . By contrast mural decoration was a continuing concern of English artists and architects during the second half of the 19th century." (Dorment, *Decoration*: p. 14) He speculates that artist and vestryman Elihu Vedder (1836–1923), along with Street, may have suggested offering the commission to

Burne-Jones. It is clear that the friendship between Burne-Jones and Street dated back to at least the mid-eighteen-fifties through the common link of William Morris (1834–1896), who was at that time articled to Street.

In her charming and perceptive *Memorials of Edward Burne-Jones,* Lady Burne-Jones wrote, "In July [1881] I find a letter containing a mention of a large scheme of mosaic which occupied Edward for years afterwards. It was for the American Protestant Episcopal Church at Rome—an incongruity not lost upon him—but the architect, Mr. G. E. Street, was a friend, and the chance of working on so large a scale was irresistible." (GB-J, II: p. 114)

The incongruity to which Lady Burne-Jones refers probably had little to do with the fact that the commission was from an American church and a good deal to do with Burne-Jones's religious sensibilities. He was born, schooled, and formally remained an Anglican, but his acceptance of other religions, and his attraction to Roman Catholicism, were in marked contrast to the Protestant focus of Dr. Nevin. As a youth Burne-Jones had been deeply affected by the Oxford Movement, and the intellectual fire which led to John Newman's conversion to the Roman Church:

Newman's simple and lofty exhortations had sunk into [Burne-Jones's] heart, and created there such belief in the writer as to make even the secession to Rome seem an act upon which it was impossible to pass judgment, and which time alone could show whether he himself might not feel bound to follow. (GB-J, I: p. 71)

Burne-Jones never did convert to Roman Catholicism, but by the eighteen-eighties when he undertook the first of the mosaics for St. Paul's, he was looking in a wistful way towards Rome. In 1886, after the unveiling of *Christ Enthroned in the Heavenly Jerusalem,* he confided to his frequent correspondent, Frances Horner, "I will influence the mind of

Dr. Nevin to give the church to the Pope—I really want to end in that faith. Somehow it isn't a banner to rally to, but what a lovely one to have been born under." (Dorment, *Decoration*: p. 132) If the alliance of Burne-Jones with Dr. Nevin was in some ways incongruous, it nonetheless produced the most ambitious single undertaking of the artist's career, the grand cycle of mosaics for St. Paul's.

Dorment notes that before Street died in December 1881, he had given Burne-Jones the measurements and curvature of the apse from which Burne-Jones then constructed a model, now in the Victoria and Albert Museum. Street lived long enough to approve the trial sketch the artist painted inside.

It is impossible to say how closely the two men then worked together in the few months before the architect's death . . . we do know that Street's plans were modest compared to the large cycle of mosaics Burne-Jones eventually carried out. (Dorment, *Roman Mosaics*: p. 74)

"I want big things to do and vast spaces," Burne-Jones wrote, prior to accepting the commission for St. Paul's, "and for common people to see them and say Oh!—only Oh!" (GB-J, II: p. 13) For the love of vast spaces he made plans to cover all the walls from roof to floor with mosaics. "On one wall there is a space of forty feet sheer down where I mean to shoot Lucifer and his knights out of a glittering heaven." (GB-J, II: p. 159) This dazzling drama was part of Burne-Jones's original theme for St. Paul's Within the Walls—The Fall of the Rebel Angels and the Fall of Man. It was never executed, although at a later time he made an easel painting of the subject. The interrupted spaces of the west wall, the place where Burne-Jones intended to place the work, were in any event probably not suitable.

It is extraordinary that over the fourteen years during which the mosaics were in process, Burne-Jones never visited the workshop in Venice, nor the site, nor installation in Rome. To offset the barriers of language and distance, the artist in England used an ingenious, though laborious, system of communication with the artisans in Italy. Lady Burne-Jones wrote that without the counsel and friendship of William Morris the task might surely have been defeating:

It would be impossible to describe the anxiety and labour connected with the mosaic. Edward and Morris used to give part of their Sunday morning time to sorting out colors used by the Venezia-Murano Company from a cabinet of tesserae . . . they made duplicate lists of the numbers on the tesserae, which when the work began to be executed, formed a means of communication with the workmen [who had a duplicate cabinet of tesserae in Murano]. (GB-J, II: pp. 141–42)

In the pastel study for *The Annunciation,* the numbered instructions for tesserae are clearly penciled in the margins, along with notes to strive for particular effects.

No actual cartoons remain for the choir decoration at St. Paul's, for they are covered by the mosaics themselves. As final preparation of the sketches, Burns-Jones drew cartoons to measure for the location, on which he carefully indicated the tesserae numbers. At Venice the cartoons were divided into sections in such a manner that a number of workmen with a range of experience could temporarily mount the tesserae onto the cartoon surfaces. The sections with this paste-up of mosaic were then reassembled and checked for effect and for necessary changes. If all was well, the cartoon was again divided into manageable sections and sent to St. Paul's for permanent installation in cement.

The British academic painter Sir Lawrence Alma-Tadema, a close friend of Burne-Jones, acted as agent to carry the cartoons for *Christ Enthroned in the Heavenly Jerusalem* to Venice. Thomas Rooke, Burne-Jones's studio assistant, pupil, and friend from the eighteen-sixties, then went to the factory, as did Nevin at least once, to check the work in progress. Burne-Jones was painstaking in his pursuit of particular effects and above all wished to avoid any suggestion of mechanical regularity. In a letter to Signor Castellani, director of the St. Paul's mosaic project for the Venezia-Murano Company, he wrote in the spring of 1884:

I cannot repeat and insist on this point [too much] that the tesserae should not be driven up close to each other but that a good reasonable space should be left of mortar between them—and that the tesserae should often be rounded at the edges a little and triangular bits here and there used . . . to avoid the mechanical look of much modern mosaic. (Dorment, *Decoration*: p. 262).

The initial difficulties, dissolving into "a very Babel of confusion" according to Lowrie, are recorded in an anguished yet amusing letter from Burne-Jones to Rooke concerning a trial angel for the apse vault:

O Rookie,—scold them, pitch into them, bully them, curse and refrain not—otherwise I must, late as it is, give it all up. You see they don't copy my outline, they don't keep my colours told them, so what the devil can I do? . . . what can I do more than mark the tesserae, and what less can they do than not read my instructions? First and foremost when the ----thing is up, you must be able to see it—TELL THEM THAT—you must know what it is about. . . . it is heartrending work—they are close to the best mosaic [sic] in the world and they can turn out this—have I bewildered them? (GB-J, II: pp. 142–43)

Fortunately as the work progressed so did the collaboration. Signor Castellani was soon writing:

I really see we shall understand perfectly well each other and our work will proceed in such way as to satisfy you. Your coloured angel was admired very much and with the assistance of Dr. Nevin we examined and studied carefully every part of it . . . thank you for the great pain you took in making this beautiful coloured angel in which we could see the perfect illustration of your ideas. (GB-J, II: p. 144)

The apse mosaic was unveiled on Christmas Day 1885. There is no record of its reception, but a letter from Burne-Jones to Nevin shortly thereafter indicates that he was ready to continue with mosaics for the church as soon as Nevin could raise funds. By 1886 he was in fact making sketches (never to be executed for the church) for the west wall.

All but four of the known pencil sketches for the arches, choir, and entrance wall are in what Burne-Jones called the "Secret Book of Designs," inscribed "EBJ 1885." The sketchbook was left by him to the British Museum. The design for the apse mosaic was completed before Burne-Jones began to use the new sketchbook.

In the spring of 1888 Burne-Jones sent to Rome studies for *The Annunciation,* and perhaps a design for *The Tree of Life* as well. Although *The Annunciation* was the first to be translated into mosaic, the sequence of drawings in the sketchbook indicates that the artist designed *The Tree of Life* first. In 1890 he sent the cartoons for *The Annunciation* to Venice, and the mosaic was prepared sometime before the 12 May 1892 meeting of the Vestry. The minutes record an awkward situation arising from lack of funds; the resolution of the problem was referred to Dr. Nevin:

The Rector states that the mosaic for the APSES [sic] of the church was finished after the design made by Burne-Jones, and that the company had expressed the wish to put it in place and wait for payment until someone should be found to give the money for it. The Vestry refused to assume responsibility for it, but authorized Dr. Nevin to make any arrangement with the company he should think advisable, on the condition it should bind itself by agreement in legal form not to ask for payment before the money for that purpose should be received, however long a time might elapse . . . If the mosaic is put up it is understood that it will be covered until paid for.

This particular financial crisis was solved by Mrs. Hickson Field in exchange for Nevin's advice on completing the Palazzo Brancaccio, a vast residence on the grounds of the Golden House of Nero on the Esquiline Hill. The palazzo, begun before Mr. Field died in April 1888, remained only half built for several years until Dr. Nevin agreed to oversee its completion.

On 12 May 1893 Burne-Jones wrote Castellani that he had sent off full-sized cartoons and a small sketch in color for, The Tree of Life "more than a fortnight earlier." On 21 November the building archives of St. Paul's records payment for transport of mosaics from Venice to Rome, and on 18 November 1894 the mosaics for both The Annunciation and The Tree of Life were unveiled.

The setting of Burne-Jones's Annunciation is an unconventional one—an unfamiliar desert location. It is probably a synthesis of several sources. Richard Dorment cites precedents for the desert setting in Islamic and Byzantine art and in ancient legends, including the apocryphal Book of James (XI:I): "And she took the pitcher and went forth to fill it with water, and lo a voice saying: 'Hail, thou who are highly favored; the Lord is with thee . . .'" Burne-Jones was probably also familiar with the 84th psalm, appointed for the second Sunday after Christmas, which contrasts the barren world of the unbeliever with the sustaining vision of the pilgrim:

Happy are the people whose strength is in you! Whose hearts are set on the pilgrim's way. Those who go through the desolate valley will find it a place of springs, for the early rains have covered it with pools of water . . .

This, the most prominent of the mosaics, is unfortunately the least successful, awkward and flat by contrast with The Tree of Life. The odd spills of water are as distracting as

Gabriel's shadow and seem more like spilled meringue than refreshing springs. Burne-Jones was fully aware of the short-comings of *The Annunciation* and wrote a plaintive letter to Castellani on 20 October 1890, reporting that he had finished the cartoons that day and would send them directly to Italy:

I know that my cartoons could have been better if I had been well—but I was weak and tired at the time, and the height I had to work made me hurry too much when I felt faint . . . (Dorment, *Decoration*: p. 273)

The mosaic was not executed for a year and a half, but as the cartoons remained in Venice during this period the artist probably never attempted to make any changes.

The Tree of Life, which Burne-Jones originally called *The Tree of Forgiveness,* was, on the other hand, his favorite of the four mosaics. In writing of it to a friend, his tone is both proud and defensive:

I doubt if you will care for it—perhaps you will . . . It's a mystical thing—Christ hanging with outspread arms but not crucified: the cross is turned into a big tree all over leaves, and the stems of the tree are gold. Everything is done to make it not a picture, and the severe limitations of mosaic are all obeyed and observed. . . . I am doing my best, but it isn't a picture and few will understand it. (GB-J, II: p. 159)

In fact, the suggestive elements and overlapping images of *The Tree of Life* seem to speak clearly. Both Lowrie and Dorment have plausibly interpreted the work as uniting three subjects in one: the *cause* of Man's Fall (the sin of Adam and Eve—for this purpose the tree becomes the Tree of Knowl-edge); the *effect* of the Fall (the loss of innocence and the expulsion from the Garden of Eden); and the *remedy* after the Fall (the coming of Christ and his sacrifice for mankind, with the tree now seen as the Tree of Life). The final one of eleven trial designs for this mosaic in the so-called "Secret Book of

Designs" carries the inscription from St. John: "In the World you will have tribulation, but trust me for I have overcome the World." This text is inscribed in Latin on the span of the arch below the mosaic.

The two arch mosaics were the last to be placed during the lifetime of either Nevin or Burne-Jones. When Burne-Jones died in 1898 he had completed sketches for the final mosaic in the vertical wall of the apse, *The Earthly Paradise,* or *Church Militant,* as Nevin called it. Work on this final mosaic was reinitiated in 1905 by Dr. Nevin, who undertook to pay for the mosaic himself. When Nevin died the following year, his heirs agreed to carry on with his financial commitment, and the mosaic was unveiled on 1 December 1907.

It had been Nevin's idea that this final mosaic commemorate several (but not all) parishioners as well as a number of friends and public figures whom he particularly admired. The idea of introducing portraits into such a work was an historic one, drawn straight from a long and pious tradition. It was not, however, an easy task for Thomas Rooke (who accepted the commission with reluctance) to execute nor a tactful one to explain. Cautiously anticipating the ill feeling that indeed followed, the Vestry notes of 1906 recapitulated the assignment as it was specified to Rooke: he was not to emphasize the element of portraiture, nor was he to introduce any portraits for either the angels or the ascetics, nor "to be at pains to make the others too prominent." Dr. Lowrie, who always enjoyed sharing an observation, commented in his history of the church, "I wonder if [earlier religious portraiture] caused so much jealousy as here? Some were angry because they were left out, some because they were given an inconspicuous place." (Lowrie, *Fifty Years*: p. 101) We may wonder why Nevin never included a portrait of the architect, George Edmund Street; Nevin's own was added on the instruction of Dr. Lowrie.

Rooke's work on *The Earthly Paradise* must have been an exacting trial in many ways. Since his early days as assistant to Burne-Jones he had earned an artistic reputation in his own right for architectural and landscape views. He nonetheless felt hesitant to implement Burne-Jones's sketches for *The Earthly Paradise*. Nevin, on the other hand, was growing old. Conscious of age and diminishing health, he was impatiently anxious to carry out this final mosaic for the choir. In his first letter to Rooke in December 1905, he prefaces his appeal for the artist's cooperation: "Between sickness and blindness I have had a pretty hard life since I met you in Burne-Jones's studio and had to suspend all aggressive work in carrying forward the decoration of my church . . ." A few weeks later he adds a different sort of pressure to a business correspondence:

I must have some more distinct idea of what your idea of this work might cost. The Church has no foundation—no funds from House— I have to beg for every penny put into it and for the last two years it has been able to pay me only 60 percent of my nominal salary of 500 pounds . . . (Dorment, *Decoration*: pp. 277, 280)

Rooke made at least 111 studies to complete *The Earthly Paradise* and took the extraordinary step of hiding these sketches under the floorboards of his studio in Bedford Park, London. They were only discovered—along with dozens of other drawings—in 1972 by Thomas Hancock, then the occupant of the house. The drawings for St. Paul's have been catalogued by Richard Dorment in his dissertation.

Dr. Lowrie gave the cost of the four parts of the Burne-Jones mosaic cycle in round figures. Neither these figures nor the Vestry notes nor building committee records are clearly itemized, and we do not know just how the expense was divided among artist, fabrication, and installation. The total figure for the apse mosaic came to $10,000, the two arches together were another $10,000, and the lower mosaic, $13,000.

Dr. Nevin resigned in 1906, having given more than half his life to St. Paul's Within the Walls, and to Rome and Italy beyond that. We catch a glimpse of the social side of Nevin's Roman—and global—nature in an autobiography by David Maitland Armstrong. Armstrong, who arrived in Rome around the same time as Nevin, successfully combined the roles of painter, civil servant, vestryman of St. Paul's, and Rector's Warden; in addition, he served as the United States Consul-General for Italy at Rome for several years. Armstrong's sketch of the first rector of St. Paul's reveals several of his many facets:

Nevin had a host of warm friends and a large acquaintance among distinguished people throughout Europe. Not only was he celebrated for his genial hospitality—always giving his guests the choicest vintages, for he was one of the best judges of wine in Italy—but no man was ever more kind-hearted and generous to the poor of all denominations. . . . He was a discriminating collector of objects of art in a large way, making the most of the great opportunities he had during his long residence in Italy, which he knew from end to end. (Armstrong: pp. 183–84)

Armstrong adds the unexpected information that Nevin was an ardent hunter with an unequaled collection of heads and trophies—none of which, however, appear to have lingered behind on the rectory walls when he retired.

Nevin's successor, Walter Lowrie, was as diverse in his sweep of interests as the first rector. Unlike Nevin, however, Lowrie had developed his many facets from a scholar's background. During his lifetime he was recognized not only for his pastoral leadership but as a distinguished Christian archaeologist and theologian.

He preached his first two sermons at St. Paul's in 1899, while Dr. Nevin was on a visit to the United States. Lowrie was in Rome at the time pursuing the study of Christian antiquities, a study begun in 1895 when he was selected as one of the first Fellows of the American School of Classical Studies. A graduate of Princeton and the Princeton Theological Seminary, Lowrie was ordained in 1896 following his return from his first study period in Rome.

Lowrie and Nevin were opposites in personal habits and doctrinal attitudes yet they formed a fast friendship during the years of their acquaintance, perhaps because they were both extraordinarily verbal, titanic in energy, and devoted to St. Paul's Within the Walls. Lowrie respected what he called Nevin's "good taste, fortified by an iron resolution," which saw to it that the church "was disfigured by no whims of art." His praise for Nevin's aesthetic judgement was unqualified, and in completing the construction of the rectory and the decoration of the church, Lowrie sought to follow the guidelines established under Nevin.

When Nevin left Rome in 1906—and we can only imagine the heavy state of his heart—he traveled to Mexico, ostensibly searching for new health. He was, in fact, planning to locate a small gold mine he had inherited years earlier in order to finance his final compelling project—to gild the ceiling of St. Paul's! He died in Mexico City that same year, without achieving this goal. He had managed, however, to communicate to his successor the notion of brightening Street's original ceiling of darkly stained wood. Five years later, in collaboration with American artist George Breck, Dr. Lowrie transformed the ceiling into a "star-sprinkled heaven . . . in imitation of the ceiling of San Zeno." The background blue was chosen to match the tones in the Burne-Jones mosaic of the apse. The Breck mosaics of the interior entrance wall would later be matched to the ceiling.

Not everyone was as keen about the twinkling vaults as Lowrie. A.D. Tani ("the egregious Sig. Tani," according to

49

A memorial plaque to the rector who built St. Paul's, Dr. Robert Jenkins Nevin, was placed over the sacristy door in 1907. The intarsia designs that frame the *piscina, sedilia* and doorway are fine examples of late nineteenth-century decorative stone work.
(Photo: John G. Ross, Rome)

Lowrie) in a guide to Rome of 1925, summarized the building in a few lines:

St. Paul's is much admired for its beautiful mosaics by Burne-Jones, and its peal of bells, 23 in number which play sacred airs like the churches in Belgium, but its ugly painted ceiling detracts much from the building. (Tani: p. 9)

The George Breck Mosaics

George William Breck (1863–1920), who directed the American Academy in Rome from 1906–1909, was a mural painter by training, a vestryman of St. Paul's and a close friend of both Nevin and Lowrie. A memorial tribute to Breck in the *American Art News* of 25 December 1920, described him as a quiet, modest and unostentatious man, reliable for his tact, kindliness of heart and clarity of vision. Versatility might certainly have been added to this list of gentle qualities, for Lowrie persuaded him to undertake a diverse range of decoration for the church, and none of it mural painting.

Breck's first assignment came in 1907 when, together with an Italian sculptor named Granchelli, he designed the memorial plaque to Dr. Nevin above the sacristy door. The plaque was a gift of William H. Herriman who had earlier given the garden fence and whose wife in 1888 had given the *piscina* and *sedilia,* the water basin and recessed seating on the south side of the chancel. (At least a part of the decorative stone inlay and carving on this south wall, a fine example of work of its kind, was the gift in 1902 of a Mr. Fahnestock, probably William Fahnestock, New York financier and Episcopal layman. There seems to be no clear record of the designer or artisan.)

In 1910 Breck turned to ecclesiastical furniture and designed a wooden pulpit to stand in front of the north ambone which Street had intended to be used for sermons. The new pulpit was of sufficient height to loft Dr. Lowrie's voice, and presence, to the back rows of the church. Some fifty years later, Dr. Woodhams returned the sermon to its original location, relying on a microphone to carry his voice over the rumble of diesel buses on via Nazionale, and moved the wooden pulpit to the first pillar on the north aisle.

But the main challenges for Breck were the mosaic decorations for the facade and the interior west wall. He began with the exterior decoration, designing mosaics for the spaces over the main portal and around the west window. These were placed in 1909 and paid for by Daniel B. Fearing, a former parishioner from Newport, Rhode Island.

A few years earlier, Dr. Nevin had written that these were the only important decorative works for the exterior left unfinished. He had wanted to fill both areas "with mosaic representations of our Lord as 'I am the door,' and of the Four Evangelists." (Nevin: p. 261) Later, Lowrie mistakenly assigned the origin of the door theme to Burne-Jones and referred to:

a memorandum to that effect; but no design (so far as I know) was ever made. Perhaps no one but Burne-Jones could have made it. I acknowledge that I cannot in the least figure to myself how such a subject might be represented pictorially. (Lowrie, *Fifty Years*: pp. 114–15)

The tympanum mosaic, as ordered by Lowrie and designed by Breck, represents St. Paul in Rome under "benevolent surveillance"—house arrest. He is seated in a pleasantly curtained room, speaking to his scribe and to a rapt guard. When the mosaic was completed, Lowrie complained that the head of St. Paul had the look of a Methodist minister. Breck modified and softened the expression later when he was working on the mosaics of the inner wall.

The Latin inscription of the tympanum is from St. Paul's letter to the Philippians (1:15–18), "the most magnanimous [words]," Lowrie wrote, "that priest, prophet, or preacher ever uttered in the conflict of religious strife . . ." He gives the following translation:

Some indeed preach Christ even of envy and strife; and some also of good will: the one do it of love, knowing that I am set for the defence of the gospel: but the other proclaim Christ of faction, not sincerely, thinking to raise up affliction for me in my bonds. *What then? only that in every way whether in pretence or in truth, Christ is proclaimed! and therein I rejoice, yea, and will rejoice. . . .* (Lowrie, *Fifty Years*: pp. 121–22)

The Latin reads: DUM OMNI MODO SIVE PER OCCASIONEM SIVE PER VERITATEM CHRISTUS ANNUNTIETUR ET IN HOC GAUDEO SED ET GAUDEBO.

The discord between Peter and Paul was of the greatest interest to Lowrie: "There has never been a schism in the Church more sharply marked than this." (Lowrie, *Fifty Years:* p. 121) In *Ss. Peter and Paul in Rome* he closely examines the roots of the controversy, and even more closely the means to the eventual reconciliation among the followers.

"In those days," Lowrie wrote, "Paul was as intolerant of Peter as Peter ever was of Paul." (Lowrie, *Peter and Paul*: p. 117) Peter and his followers accounted Mosaic Law, as observed in daily Jewish Life, an essential tradition to carry along into Christianity. The far-flung Gentiles, however, as diverse in geography as in culture, shared no such Judaic memories, and Paul resisted forcing these older rituals and customs upon the new Christians.

In resifting the archaeological evidence, Lowrie supported the belief that the bodies of both saints, martyred separately in Rome under Nero, were brought together for safekeeping in the catacombs beneath the basilica of San Sebastiano on the Appia Antica some two hundred years later, during the Christian persecution under the Emperor Valerian. The reconciliation of the opposed groups of followers after the martyrdoms "was a striking witness not only to the power of Christianity, but to [Peter's and Paul's] personal faith and their common faithfulness to Christ." (Lowrie, *Peter and Paul*: p. 105)

In a reflective afterthought, Lowrie later wished that the tympanum words expressed a less "belligerent pacifism"; nonetheless when they were carved in 1909 they marked a giant step forward from the intransigence towards the Roman Church that characterized the parish of 1870.

Concerning the decoration at the corners of the west window, an 1875 perspective by Street shows what may be either a mosaic or a low relief sculpture. The watercolor perspective was very kindly given to St. Paul's in 1979 by the Very Reverend Francis B. Sayre, Jr., Dr. Nevin's great nephew (and grandson of President Woodrow Wilson.) As carried out by Breck, the mosaic decoration shows each of the four Evangelists clasping a book bearing his own name. The symbolic representations are the visions that appear to Ezekiel (1:4) and are again mentioned in the Revelation of John (4:6). Dr. Lowrie noted that the attributes that are now traditional in art for the Evangelists were first arranged according to the series of the Gospels in the fourth-century apse of Santa Pudenziana, a source for several elements in the Breck mosaics. He gives the final cost of the facade mosaics as $6,000.

Breck began the interior mosaics in 1911, perhaps initially working from a preliminary set of sketches by Elihu Vedder, who at seventy-five was too old to carry out the work. According to the Vestry Minutes, Vedder received 1,000 lire in November 1912 for his services in connection with the west wall.

The money for this final mosaic decoration of St. Paul's, which would run to $14,000, was given jointly in 1911 by the financier and art collector J. Pierpont Morgan (whose father had earlier given the apse mosaic), and his longtime friend William H. Herriman. Both men were generous donors to St. Paul's over a period of years, and after J. P. Morgan's death in 1913 his son was to carry down to a third generation a financial commitment to the church.

These two mosaics, *The Creation of the World* and *The Adoration of the Magi,* are intended to be seen as a whole, reading from top to bottom, but architectural interruptions as well as the contrasting designs, work to keep them apart. The Creation, with Adam waking among the animals of the peaceable kingdom, forms an upper section that has the brightness and austerity of surrealism. It is strangely still yet awesomely energized by the hand of God and the complexity of the heavens. For the representations of Bethlehem and Jerusalem, Lowrie and Breck again drew on Santa Pudenziana. This upper scene has never received the attention it deserves, partly because it is high above the floor, poorly lighted and always obscure, and partly because it is assumed to suffer from comparison with the Burne-Jones mosaics of the choir.

The Christmas text, bringing together both the magi and shepherds, was a challenge to work into the arched spaces over the main portal, and the solution as it stands was received as a triumph of ingenuity. The paired colonnettes, rather than dividing as barriers, act as sectional frames within a whole. This is a popular and pleasing narrative scene, rich in a variety of deep colors, and uniting a number of traditional elements from the Nativity and Epiphany stories.

The work on these final mosaics went relatively swiftly compared to the seventeen years Burne-Jones was occupied with the decoration of the east end of the church. But even

The mosaics of the west wall by George William Breck, installed in 1913, combine the stories of the creation of the world with the nativity and adoration of the Magi and shepherds. Eight Roman martyrs surround Christ in the rose window by Clayton and Bell, 1875. (Photo: John G. Ross, Rome)

such a gentle man as Breck was unable to avoid conflict, this time with the Vestry. In a testy note, dated simply 1913 but probably written in the fall, he was roundly scolded for the continued presence of scaffolding in the church (probably left up from the 1911 campaign to paint the ceiling and to be used in installing the new mosaics). In unequivocal terms the Vestry stated that it wanted the scaffolding out of the way during "the Winter season . . . after Easter the mosaics may be put in place at Mr. Breck's own risk and expense." The threat evidently was effective, for the mosaics were unveiled on Christmas Day of 1913.

Street's Tiles

The Breck mosaics were the last of several major modifications to the interior of St. Paul's as Street had originally planned it. Indeed, the mosaics are far more extensive than the single one Street discussed with Burne-Jones for the apse semi-dome. The alternating brick and marble bands, which Street ordered and saw in place over the nave and choir arches, were replaced in 1894 by *The Annunciation* and *The Tree of Life*. Around 1907, the lancet windows of the lower apse were closed to make way for the rich sweep of figures of *The Earthly Paradise*—a change from relative simplicity to glittering complexity. Similarly, the painting of the ceiling, while pleasing and effectively done, is another decorative distraction where Street had planned somber obscurity.

The striking ceramic tiles that form a dado along the interior nave walls suffer particularly from these various enrichments. The history of these tiles—handsomely assertive, with few colors and bold leaf patterns—has become strangely confused in a relatively short time, perhaps because of the controversy they have provoked. Lowrie felt they were a

Street's forceful interior was designed to have little additional decoration beyond the stained glass windows and the mosaic in the
apse semi–dome which can be only dimly seen here. The photograph
dates to before 1894, when the Burne-Jones *Annunciation* and *Tree
of Life* were installed above the choir and chancel arches. The apse
windows were removed in 1907 to make way for *The Earthly Paradise*. The capitals and moldings have not yet been carved.
(Photo: Alinari, Rome)

jarring note in Nevin's otherwise harmonious decorative scheme for St. Paul's.

Over the years the tiles have often been attributed to William Morris since they have the assurance and vigor associated with Burne-Jones's friend and colleague. According to Dorment's finding, however, they were designed by the architect and executed by Clayton and Bell, the firm that made the stained glass windows. It is actually not surprising that they are by Street; one of the strengths of his buildings is that he designed virtually everything himself. Richard Norman Shaw, a dominant figure among Victorian architects, leader in the Arts and Crafts movement, and onetime apprentice to Street, wrote that the students in Street's office were never permitted to design so much as a keyhole. After Street's death Shaw reaffirmed the point: "The charm of his work is that when looking at it you may be certain it is entirely his own, and this applies to the small detail as to the general conception." (Street, A. E.: p. 283)

Viewing the tiles, which are arranged to correspond to the architectural rhythms of the side aisles, it should be borne in mind that Street intended little decoration for the church beside the furniture of the chancel, the stained glass windows, and the apse mosaic in the semi-dome. He deliberately created the facing of tile along the length of the two side aisles to form a rich and unifying band around the lower walls, framing a contemplative space for meditation and worship.

Baptistry and Canterbury Chapel

In addition to the Breck mosaics, Lowrie undertook two other major changes in the interior. The first was in the baptistry. Lowrie carried out earlier plans to install marble sheathing on the lower baptistry walls below the inscription

The baptistry, which supports the bell tower, was sheathed in a bold marble, *fior di pesca brecciata,* by the second rector, Dr. Walter Lowrie. The stained glass window is part of the series done for St. Paul's by the distinguished London firm of Clayton and Bell. The Victorian baptismal font, placed during the 1880s, was the gift of George W. Wurts from Philadelphia. (Photo: John G. Ross, Rome)

The Chapel of St. Augustine of Canterbury was dedicated in November 1976. The bronze and gold aumbry and four mosaic wall tiles were designed for the chapel by Elizabeth A. B. Jones. The early medieval relief cross is from the collection of Dr. Nevin.
(Photo: John G. Ross, Rome)

to John David Wolfe and his daughter, Catherine Lorillard Wolfe, outstanding supporters of the building program. The work was accomplished in 1910, using the boldly veined marble called *fior di pesca brecciata.*

The second major innovation was in what is now the Canterbury Chapel. Here, at the head of the north aisle, he put to use the leftover stone from the baptistry to construct an altar, a project that had been considered since Dr. Nevin's time. Lowrie's inspiration to create much out of little—he covered the walls with damask and suspended an oriental rug as an altar screen—came to him from similar chapels at the Benedictine monastery of Sant' Anselmo on the Aventine. He enjoyed the idea that "in matters of taste the Benedictines were the Episcopalians of the Roman church." (Lowrie, *Fifty Years:* p. 45) Several years later the walls were sheathed in green *cipollino,* and the inscription added in memory of Ambassador and Mrs. Thomas Nelson Page, in Italy during the years of the First World War. A section of Street's controversial tile may possibly still be underneath the *cipollino* wall.

The chapel underwent a third modification under Woodhams in 1976, when it was prepared for dedication to St. Augustine of Canterbury. The dedication to St. Augustine was intended as a visible statement by St. Paul's of a program to restate and re-energize the mission of the branches of the Anglican Communion. Only a few changes were made to the existing chapel. Most important was the commission of a bronze and gilt tabernacle for the altar from professional medallist Elizabeth A. B. Jones (1935–), American artist resident in Rome and parishioner of St. Paul's. The gradine, or raised marble step at the back of the altar stone on which the cross and candlesticks normally stand, was sawn in two and the halves separated to make a space for the tabernacle.

Elizabeth Jones also designed four mosaic shields that were placed at this time to the sides of the altar. Anglican bishops,

English-speaking clergy in Rome, and representatives of His Holiness Pope Paul VI gathered for the dedication. The statement of Anglican ecumenism served as a prelude to the opening the following year of the Great Doors of Christan Unity, dedicated to the memory of Pope John XXIII.

The Rectory

Among the tasks inherited by Lowrie was the completion of the rectory. This handsome building, with its Venetian Gothic facade on via Napoli, had a long and fitful thirty-four year building history, due almost entirely to the unpredictable arrival of gifts to the building fund. Street had included the rectory in the perspective drawing of 1875, indicating that he considered it an integral part of the church. The one extant working drawing, however, in the collection of the Royal Institute of British Architects, is not dated until 1880.

During that summer, the rector had collected $8,500 toward the new building, with another $1,000 promised by subscription, according to the Vestry notes of 9 November 1880. This was a sufficient portion of the architect's building estimate of $17,000 for work to begin. (Lowrie figured the final cost of the completed building to have been close to $65,000.)

In 1880, construction began to a depth of three rooms behind the facade. The structure was then, as described by Lowrie,

"a towerlike construction, including the main stairway, but only half of the present study. The front [actually the flank] had soon to be lengthened by one room on the garden side in order to wedge the side wall of the church between the rectory and the campanile, thus preventing the enlargement of a crack which seriously threat-

Plans for the rectory, with its Venetian Gothic facade, were made by Street, but nearly all the work was carried out over a thirty-five year period after his death in 1881. (Photo: John G. Ross, Rome)

ened the church. This change made it impossible to carry out the original design of a cloister connecting the rectory with the church . . . (Lowrie, *Fifty Years*: p. 39)

(On the interior south wall of the church today, in the last bay before the enclosed sacristy, there is visible evidence of the closing of a doorway once planned to lead to the proposed cloister.)

Subsequently, progress on the rectory proceeded at a snail-like pace, as the records reveal. On 16 May 1891 the Vestry advised against any further building, but authorized Nevin to order the stone and hold it ready until funds were located. On 7 December of the same year, after a promise of help from William Waldorf Astor, construction proceeded once again, only to be halted within the month by order of the Municipality; the proposed plans violated the formula of the 1888 building regulations that limited the height of new buildings in Rome to three times the width of the vacant space between the neighboring buildings. (Vestry Minutes, 16 January 1892.) How the problem was resolved is not quite clear, but the new section had been roofed by the end of the year. By 1895 the remaining rectory rooms were completed, but so minimally that it took Lowrie another seven years to finish the building after his arrival in 1907. In a backstairs look at his predecessor's lifestyle, he wrote that Nevin

"continued to camp out [in the rectory] even when the whole house was built . . . . on account of the great number of works of art which he had collected the rooms which his guests saw were interesting and even splendid but he himself continued to live in what most of us would regard as discomfort . . . . He said of himself he was more at home in the saddle than in the pulpit . . . He eschewed sheets and he had a fire in only one room, though fortunately he built a rectory with thirty-two flues. (Lowrie, *Fifty Years*: pp. 39–40).

There are some fine marble details in the rectory, including the doorframe inside the via Napoli entrance and several fireplace moldings from the Palazzo Torlonia in Piazza Venezia. (The palazzo had been demolished to provide a clear view of the Victor Emmanuel Monument, and it served as a sculptural quarry for many new buildings in Rome.) The drawing-room fireplace with a chariot race of four putti carved in the lintel, was formerly attributed to the noted Danish sculptor A. B. Thorwaldsen, but recent and more modest rethinking has ascribed it to his studio in Rome.

Among the objects Nevin collected personally and left to the church are the four large fourteenth-century frescoes of saints in the rectory drawing-room or *salone*. Nevin is believed to have found them in Gubbio, where they had been removed from a small church that was turned into a stable in the early nineteenth century. Other furnishings for the *salone* were bought in 1909 with the proceeds from the sale of the library of Madama Emily Nancrede Fedeli.

During the rectorship of Canon C. A. Shreve (rector 1954–1957) a number of murals were painted in the rectory. On the top floor Spanish painter Fernando Calderon carried out a series of wall paintings as well as the Nativity scene for the dining room on the *piano nobile*. The murals in the corridor outside the dining room are by Leonard Creo, an American artist living in Rome after the Second World War.

First World War to the Present

The initial stage in the building history of St. Paul's ends with the First World War. There have been several substantial gifts since that time, including the Steinway grand piano given in 1933 by David Russell MacIver, the elevator for the rectory in 1938 by the doctors Adeline Gurd and Patty Gurd

Wilson, and an outstanding gift in 1971—proceeds from the sale of parishioner Elizabeth Woodruff's villa and its contents. Until the 1960s, however, the story of the church was principally one of maintenance rather than modification.

In 1926 Dr. Lowrie wrote sadly of post First World War changes in Rome as they affected St. Paul's:

> As a parish we still feel the effects of the war, and this long experience prompts me to wish that by a small endowment we might be protected against disaster. I am not anticipating another universal war: a temporary lull or deflection of tourist traffic might leave us stranded for a time. For the stable colony here is now smaller, I believe, than it was fifty years ago. There are not two hundred Americans living in Rome, while there are more than a hundred times as many in Paris. (Lowrie, *Fifty Years:* p. 51)

Lowrie's letter of resignation in 1930, transcribed in the Vestry notes of 25 January, deplored the fact that the number of Americans was still continuing to dwindle, and that thereby the character of his ministry had changed entirely; perhaps he also could foresee the strife ahead for Italy under Mussolini's fascist leadership.

In contrast to the sixty-one years combined tenure of Drs. Nevin and Lowrie, four rectors tended St. Paul's Within the Walls during the troubled decade, 1930–1940: Dr. Theodore Sedgwick, Canon Samuel Tyler, the Reverend Appleton Grannis, and the Reverend Hiram G. Woolfe. Finally, following Mussolini's entrance into the war on the side of the Axis, the church was closed on 26 May 1940 "until further notice," and upon the American declaration of war in December of the following year it was placed under the protection of the Swiss Legation in Rome. The church was reopened in 1943 for use of the United States Army, battling from Sicily northward through Italy in the costly offensive against German divisions. The simple pews still in use today were made at that time by the quartermaster corps from their stockpile of pine boards.

St. Paul's reorganized after the Second World War under Hillis Duggins (rector 1946–1954), whose intensive labors to repair the church after its wartime neglect, to stabilize its finances, and to rebuild the congregation contributed to the tragedy of his early death in Rome.

Since Wilbur C. Woodhams became rector in 1961 there have been several changes in the fabric of the church. In addition to transforming the crypt into the spaces of Undercroft and preparing the new Canterbury Chapel, he has redesigned the choir and chancel and installed the commemorative entrance doors.

The redesigning of the chancel, carried out in 1969 at a cost of some $2,000, was the expression of an earlier idea of Dr. Lowrie. In *Action in the Liturgy* Lowrie stated that he wanted to return to the early Roman Catholic practice of locating the altar *between* the clergy and the people, thereby reaffirming in the Holy Table the symbol of the sacramental unity of the Church. The reordering of the furniture of the chancel not only realized Dr. Lowrie's wish for reform (*not* a revolution, he emphasized), but has brought the congregation closer to the sacrament in conformity with the new liturgy.

This change was effected by shortening Street's original rail of various marbles for the *schola cantorum,* and placing the two peacock entrance gates in upright frames, spaced apart to leave a path to the altar.

The partitions for the choir stalls were removed, and, to enrich the enlarged floor space of the choir, the original encaustic tiles were brought forward from the sanctuary. The sanctuary now has a glazed terracotta floor in a traditional Roman pattern. The brass sanctuary rail has gone into storage, and the level of the sanctuary is now lowered by one step. The wooden altar, given to St. Paul's by Dr. Nevin as a memorial to his brother, Richard Cecil Nevin, was brought forward six feet. This arrangement permits the celebrant to move freely behind the altar and to prepare the Eucharist with the participating witness of the congregation. The retable was not moved, but rather lowered by removing the marble base, putting the Bishop's Chair at a visually appropriate height. The only cross now used is a memorial to the Right Reverend Stephen Fielding Bayne, Jr. (late Bishop of the Diocese of Olympia, Washington, and Executive Officer of the Anglican Communion.) The cross, designed and executed by Siracusa in 1975, was given by the Bishop's brother, Edward Ashley Bayne, Roman resident for many years, and an active leader and member of the parish of St. Paul's in the decades of the nineteen-sixties and seventies. It is carried in the procession and placed on the retable during the service.

The Bishop's Chair, which was in place for the consecration of the church in 1876, was given to St. Paul's largely by subscription from the English and Scottish churches. It originally stood in its present location behind the altar, but the retable, then higher, concealed the body of any visiting bishop and gave to his head an odd, dismembered appearance. The Reverend Theodore Sedgwick (rector 1930–1934) was sensitive to this problem and moved the chair to the north side of the apse. This, however, contradicted the ancient practice (preserved only in Rome and in a few cathedrals of southern Italy, according to Lowrie) of seating the bishop behind the Holy Table. Father Duggins knew this argument and according to the Vestry notes of 13 January 1948 requested and received permission to return the chair to its original position—reverting to the original problem. Here it remained for twenty-one years, seldom seen and less used, until the chancel was redesigned.

The choir and chancel before and after 1969. Changes are shown on
the right: three marble steps (red, white, red) now lead up from the
nave; the low marble railings to the sides of the choir entrance and
the brass sanctuary rail were removed; the sanctuary was lowered
one step; the choir stalls were put in storage and the original

sanctuary tiles brought forward and placed over the exposed
wooden floor; the organ console was moved to the north; the
altar was moved forward two meters, and the gradine lowered to
serve now as a bench and retable in front of the Bishop's Chair.
(Photos: T. Makula and John G. Ross, Rome)

By the early nineteen-seventies it had become apparent that while St. Paul's had been gaining increased appreciation for its architecture and decoration, it had at the same time been falling prey to some serious aging problems. This awareness marked the beginning of a new effort aimed at preserving the fabric of St. Paul's Within the Walls.

Among the first to recognize the need for preservation was W. Brown Morton III, a specialist in architectural restoration, who was sent to Rome by the National Park Service in 1972 as an instructor at the International Center for the Preservation and Restoration of Cultural Property. (Also an Episcopal communicant, he began preparation for his ordination while in Rome.) Drawn by the architectural quality of St. Paul's, Morton used the building as a training ground for his students. They worked together under the guidance of Bernard Feilden, preeminent in the field of British architectural restoration and at that time a visiting member of the Rome Center faculty. The building was exactingly probed and measured for evidence of deterioration and structural weakness. Following the recommendations of Feilden and Morton, Roman architect Paolo Marconi began the campaign of cleaning and repair in 1974.

Feilden and Morton's preparatory work revealed a host of problems. One of the weakest points in the church fabric is along the north side, where a florist shop, pressed against the flank of the building since the beginning of the century, has caused serious water damage; eviction of the tenant and demolition of the shop are presently not legally possible solutions. The survey found serious defects in the exterior stonework: the same French stone that proved so easy to carve on the interior was also used for exterior column capitals, bases, dentils, and thin moldings on the campanile. Extensive erosion on the south and east sides led to the recommendation that this stone be replaced by travertine. The bell supports need to be replaced, and fortunately funds are in hand for an up-dated ringing system. There is other evidence of deterioration: the stones at the top of the facade have begun for some unexplained reason to push forward; the stone cross on the roof was damaged when it blew down during a violent windstorm in 1979; the glazing of the west window at the interface of lead and stone has crumbled. The list goes on. The return from the sale of the Woodruff estate has formed the nucleus of a fund—for which other revenues are being sought—for the first major cleaning and restoration work now underway.

This building history of St. Paul's Within the Walls closes with the dedication of the commemorative doors which took place at a Festival Evensong on 28 April 1977. Assembled for the service were the reverend members of the Pontifical Secretariat for Christian Unity, led by His Eminence Johannes Cardinal Willebrands, the Archbishop of Canterbury, Frederick Donald Coggan, and five other English and American bishops. The following day, in a public ceremony in the Sistine Chapel, His Holiness Pope Paul VI received the Archbishop of Canterbury in a continuation of the fraternal encounters between the Roman and Anglican leaders, initiated by Pope John XXIII and Archbishops Fisher and Ramsey.

The idea for the doors was conceived by Dr. Woodhams in 1963, following the death of Pope John XXIII. A tribute to the Pope's Christian charity and ecumenical leadership, the doors would symbolize the figurative door Pope John opened when he received a visit in 1960 from the Most Reverend Geoffrey Fisher, Archbishop of Canterbury and the following year from the Most Reverend Arthur Lichtenberger, Presiding Bishop of the Protestant Episcopal Church of the United States. Proposing the idea of memorial doors in a parish letter of 4 June 1963, Woodhams suggested that they commemorate these historic interchanges between the Anglican and Roman churches:

I have long imagined such a door—now is the right time to go ahead because there is a reason that is perhaps the greatest reason for our little congregation being here in Rome.

Woodhams originally envisioned "two magnificent doors of clear glass and wrought iron or bronze," etched with representations of the seminal exchanges between the leaders of the Anglican and Roman churches. Looking through the glass to the interior, Christians of all denominations "could then look into the church and have a visible witness to our oneness in Christ as they see the altar and the great symbolism of the mosaic behind it."

The glass doors proved unworkable, however, and it was decided to install more traditional (and less vulnerable) doors of cast bronze. American sculptor Dimitri Hadzi (1921–), at that time resident in Rome and a long-time member of the congregation of St. Paul's, volunteered to undertake their design and execution.

To symbolize Pope John's Christian leadership and warmth of spirit on bronze doors opening into a Protestant church in the capital of Latin Christendom, was no ordinary challenge. At length, it was resolved to express Pope John's initiation of the healing of the four-hundred-year old breach between two major branches of Christianity. The doors would treat neither a particular time nor place but would record the historically fragmented church, and the renewed dream of unity.

Hadzi's voluntary offer in 1963 turned into a fourteen-year labor. He drew literally scores of sketches and prepared models in both plaster and wax as he moved from simple representational ideas to the abstract outlines on which his final statement is based. In driving around Italy to survey centuries of bronze church doors it was a curious coincidence that Hadzi was particularly struck by the twelfth-century doors of San Zeno, the church in Verona that had influenced George Edmund Street a hundred years earlier in designing St. Paul's.

From the laying of the cornerstone to the hanging of the doors, little that has occurred in the building of St. Paul's has happened by chance. The church has been shaped and modified for one hundred and ten years by attitudes that have belonged to the times, and by personalities that have belonged to the congregations of American Episcopalians in Rome. From a defiant beginning as a challenge to the singleness of the Roman Catholic Church in the Eternal City, St. Paul's Within the Walls now proclaims, in words incised in English and Italian on the framing stone of the entrance doors, the visionary message of Pope John XXIII: "That all may be one." The words are a permanent tribute, on Anglican stone, to the age of *aggiornamento* and the reawakened goal of Christian unity.

1. The cycle of mosaics for St. Paul's Within the Walls by Edward Burne-Jones, the lower register completed by Thomas Matthew Rooke. Photo: John G. Ross, Rome

2. The Burne-Jones watercolor study, c. 1888, for *The Annunciation,*
with his notations for mosaic tesserae. Photo: Courtesy Roy
Miles Gallery, London

3. The Archangel Gabriel by Edward Burne-Jones, detail from the apse semi-dome. Unveiled 25 December 1885. Photo: St. Paul's Within the Walls, Rome

4. *The Tree of Life* by Edward Burne-Jones. Unveiled 18 November 1894. Photo: John G. Ross, Rome

5. The Virgin Saints and Christian Warriors, from *The Earthly Paradise,* completed by Thomas Matthew Rooke after the design by Burne-Jones. Unveiled 1 December 1907. Photo: St. Paul's Within the Walls, Rome

6. West window by Clayton and Bell, 1875, and mosaics by George
William Breck, 1913. Photo: St. Paul's Within the Walls, Rome

7. Section of the nave wall tiles by George Edmund Street, c. 1875.
Photo: John G. Ross, Rome

8. Peacock gates which originally closed the choir entrance, c. 1880.
Photo: John G. Ross, Rome

9. The great bronze doors by Dimitri Hadzi were opened 28 April 1977. The tympanum mosaic is by George William Breck, 1909. Photo: Raffaele Baldi, Rome

II

A GUIDE TO THE CHURCH

A Guide to the Church

The Burne-Jones Mosaics

THE INSTALLATION of the four mosaics by Edward Burne-Jones (see pp. 36–47) spanned a period of over twenty years. The sequence of their unveiling and the names of their donors are as follows:

25 DECEMBER 1885   *Christ Enthroned in the Heavenly Jerusalem*. Semi-dome of the apse. The gift of Junius S. Morgan.

18 NOVEMBER 1894   *The Annunciation* and *The Tree of Life*. Over the two arches of the choir and chancel. The gifts of Mrs. Hickson Field; *The Annunciation* a memorial to her husband (d. 18 April 1888), *The Tree of Life* to Mary Eleanor Field (d. 20 December 1865).

1 DECEMBER 1907   *The Earthly Paradise*, or *Church Militant*. The initial design by Burne-Jones was carried out by Thomas Rooke. The gift of the rector, the Reverend Robert J. Nevin, and his heirs.

The unifying theme of the four mosaics is the Redemption of Man through the coming and sacrifice of Christ. The arrangement follows a Byzantine plan with Christ the Pantocrator or Holy Ruler in the highest space of the apse; in the secondary zones—the arches—are narrative scenes from the life of Christ, the Annunciation and Crucifixion; and in the lowest zone—the vertical wall of the apse—is the holy body of apostles, martyrs, virgin saints, and others.

Christ Enthroned in the Heavenly Jerusalem takes many traditional elements from the Book of Revelation. A beardless Christ raises his right hand in blessing while his left clasps the orb, the globe of the earth, with an inner landscape of mountains and fields. Seraphim and cherubim surround Christ's throne, and above his head is the host of angels holding their heavenly instruments. His feet rest on the rainbow that arches over the four streams of the River of Life, in which the early church perceived a reference to the four Gospels. The crenellated walls of the New Jerusalem rise behind him.

In front of the six gates stand some of the archangels with their attributes. To the far left is Uriel, guardian of the sun; next is Michael with spear and shield; the dark rectangle of the empty gate, framed in red, was Lucifer's place before his fall; Gabriel stands on Christ's left hand holding the lily of the Annunciation; beside him is Chemuel, the cup-bearer, with a goblet and pilgrim's staff; to the far right stands Zophiel, guardian of the moon. One can imagine that the remaining archangels would be standing in the gates of the circle if it were completed.

The inscription beneath was not planned by Burne-Jones and was added after his death. From the middle, reading to the left in Hebrew, are the opening words of Genesis: *In the beginning God created the heavens and the earth*; in Greek, reading to the right, are the opening words of the Gospel of St. John: *In the beginning was the Word, and the Word was with God.*

On the "triumphal" or choir arch is *The Annunciation* represented in an unconventional desert setting. It is probably dawn, the time of a new beginning, with the low light casting shadows of Gabriel and of Mary. The Virgin, draped in a white garment stands with her hands clasped to her chest, her head bent towards the archangel in an attitude both humble and attentive. Gabriel, on the left, hovers a few inches above the ground. His white-draped figure, framed by massive blue and lavender wings, is inclined towards the Virgin. To her right is the water jar she has brought to fill. In the lower left of the mosaic a pelican, an early symbol of Christ, plucks at its breast to draw blood to feed its young. The parched landscape with its miraculous pools of water may be seen as the wasteland before the coming of Christ; it anticipates the greening world seen in the orb of the mosaic of the Heavenly Jerusalem.

The Latin inscription on the arch of *The Annunciation* begins with Gabriel's greeting (Luke 1:28): *Hail thou that art highly favored, the Lord is with thee,* and continues with Mary's reply (Luke 1:38) *Behold the handmaid of the Lord; be it unto me according to thy word.*

The Tree of Life, on the arch over the chancel, is carefully balanced, rich in color and rhythm, and a synthesis of references. It combines the theme of the fall of Adam and Eve and their labor with that of Christ's sacrifice and forgiveness of man's sins. In front of the Tree of Life Christ is suspended with outstretched arms, though there is no visible cross. This muscular glowing man is not Christ the excruciated, but Christ the willing sacrifice, a heroic figure, the risen Lord. The lush Tree of Life rises from a multiplicity of trunks twined together and spreads in a wide circle of leafy limbs. To the left and right of Christ stand Adam and Eve—man and woman—humanity. Adam, looking towards Christ, stands with his palms pressed together in the attitude of prayer, his long garment caught up by a belt to free him for his labor. To Adam's left are bound sheaves of wheat, the fruit of his labor and traditional references to the Eucharist and the sacrifice of Christ. Eve, represented as Charity, holds one child while the other clings to her knee; to her right the lily of the Annunciation springs into bloom from a stem of thistles. The olive and mulberry trees of Italy are in the lowest corners of the scene. The Latin inscription below was written by Burne-Jones beside the final design for this mosaic: *In the World you will have tribulation, but trust me for I have overcome the world.* (John 16:33)

Nine years after the death of Burne-Jones, Thomas Matthew Rooke completed the vertical wall of the apse, working from a Burne-Jones drawing with notes to identify various of the saints and groups of figures. This lower register of the apse wall had attracted singular attention even before the unveiling in 1907, for the faces of most of the figures are contemporary portraits of parishioners, friends, and public figures selected by Dr. Nevin.

This mosaic, the last of the four designed by Burne-Jones for St. Paul's, is called variously *The Earthly Paradise, The Church Triumphant,* or *Church Militant* (the last title favored by Dr. Nevin). It is separated from *The Heavenly Jerusalem* above by a graceful line of angels dividing the heavenly waters of salvation from the oceans of the earth. The Byzantine church in the background recalls St. Mark's in Venice. There are five groups of figures, each of which represents a traditional Christian role or expression. To the far left are male and female Ascetics, emerging like hermits from their rocky shelters with hands stretched upwards towards Christ in Glory. St. Francis is the one clearly identifiable figure in this group, in which Dr. Nevin specified that there should be no portraits. The second group from the left represents the Matron Saints, fully draped in garments of various hues, standing at the edge of the desert. Mary Magdalene, identified by the ointment jar in her hand, alone stands within the fertile landscape which is represented in the manner of early

Christian mosaics from Ravenna. Martha, to her left, has a collection of keys hanging at her waist.

The central group of male figures is composed of five Fathers of the Greek Eastern Church and four Fathers of the Latin Western. In the center is St. Paul, wearing a chasuble, the vestment commonly worn throughout the Catholic Church for the celebration of the Eucharist. The martyred Virgin Saints, with their identifying attributes, file in from the hills to the right: St. Catherine with her wheel, St. Barbara with a tower, St. Cecilia with an organ, St. Dorothea with her roses, St. Agnes with her lamb. The final group, composed of mounted Christian warriors, enters from the right against a backdrop of laurel, whose leafy branches since antiquity have been twined into wreathes for the heads of heroes. The five warriors that can be identified by their shields are, from left to right: St. George of England, St. James of Spain, St. Patrick of Ireland, St. Andrew of Scotland, and St. Denis of France. St. Longinus, whose spear pierced the side of Christ, is alone on foot.

The following portrait identifications were verified by Rooke for Dr. Lowrie, who published them in his 1926 history of St. Paul's. The expanded biographical information was for the most part collected by Richard Dorment. The identifications are numbered to read from left to right within each group:

THE ASCETICS OR HERMIT SAINTS

There are no portraits.

THE MATRON SAINTS

1. Martha is Catherine Lorillard Wolfe (1828–1887), American philanthropist and patroness of the arts. She was a major

A key to the portraits in the *The Earthly Paradise*. The four groups read from left to right and are numbered sequentially within each group. Identifications are on pages 83, 85–87

benefactor of the American Episcopal Church and donated the bell tower of St. Paul's Within the Walls.

2. Mrs. William Bacon Stevens, second wife of William Bacon Stevens (1815–1887), Bishop of Pennsylvania and prelate in charge of American churches in Europe.

3. The only other portrait in this group is of a Mrs. Beckett, evidently a friend of Nevin's, about whom nothing is known.

THE FATHERS OF THE CHURCH

1. St. Columba is Alonzo Potter (1800–1865), Bishop of Pennsylvania from 1845 to 1865, and first clergyman to hold an Episcopal service in Rome.

2. St. Gregory Nazianus is William H. Herriman, a generous donor to St. Paul's and active in its affairs, who lived in Rome with his wife after 1865.

3. St. Athanasius is the Reverend Robert Jenkins Nevin (1839–1906), the builder of St. Paul's.

4. St. Basil is George Perkins Marsh (1801–1882), a lawyer, diplomat, and scholar, appointed by President Lincoln as first United States minister to the united Kingdom of Italy, a post he held from 1861 to 1881.

5. St. John Chrysostom is Sir Edward Coley Burne-Jones (1833–1898), who created the grand cycle of mosaics for St. Paul's.

6. St. Paul in the center is not a portrait.

7. St. Augustine is a portrait of Richard Cecil Nevin, Dr. Robert Nevin's brother, who was also a clergyman.

8. Pope St. Gregory I is Archibald Campbell Tait (1811–1882), former headmaster of Rugby School, who became

Bishop of London in 1856 and Archbishop of Canterbury in 1869.

9. St. Jerome is Dr. Johann Joseph Ignatius von Döllinger (1799–1890), a German priest and professor who fought against the proclamation of the doctrine of Papal Infallibility. He defied the Pope on this issue and was excommunicated.

10. St. Ambrose is Junius Spencer Morgan (1813–1890), founder of the banking "House of Morgan," father of the financial titan John Pierpont Morgan (1837–1913), and grandfather of J. P. Morgan the younger (1867–1943). Junius S. Morgan's portrait was included because he donated the mosaic in the dome of the apse. His son and grandson were also vigorous supporters of the Episcopal Church and generous benefactors of St. Paul's.

THE VIRGIN SAINTS

1. St. Catherine (with the wheel) is Mrs. Henry Codman Potter, second wife of Henry Codman Potter (1835–1908), Bishop of New York and son of Alonzo Potter.

2. St. Barbara (with the tower) is Georgiana, Lady Burne-Jones (1840–1920), wife of the painter.

3. St. Cecilia (with the organ) is Mary Dahlgren Astor (d. 1894), wife of financier William Waldorf Astor (1848–1919). Astor, who began life as an American and ended it as a British Viscount, was appointed by President Arthur as minister to Italy (1882–85), succeeding George Perkins Marsh.

4. St. Dorothea (with the roses) is Mrs. Mackail, daughter of William Morris.

5. St. Agnes (with the lamb) is Gwendolin Story.

THE CHRISTIAN WARRIORS

1. St. George is General Winfield Scott Hancock (1824–1886), Civil War general famed for his leadership at Gettysburg, who was the Democratic nominee for president in 1880 but narrowly lost the election to James A. Garfield.

2. St. James of Spain is the Italian patriot Giuseppe Garibaldi (1807–1882).

3. St. Patrick is Ulysses Simpson Grant (1822–1885), leader of the Union forces in the Civil War and eighteenth President of the United States.

4. St. Andrew is Abraham Lincoln (1809–1865), sixteenth President of the United States.

5. St. Longinus, the footsoldier with a spear, is believed to be Thomas M. Rooke (1842–1942) who completed this mosaic after the death of Burne-Jones.

6. St. Denis is Henry White (1850–1927), American Ambassador to Italy from 1905 to 1907.

7. The sixth mounted soldier does not have the attributes of a specific saint. The portrait is of Père Hyacinthe (1827–1912) born Charles Loyson in Orleans, France. An eloquent and popular preacher at Notre Dame in Paris, he defied the Pope on the doctrine of Papal Infallibility, was excommunicated in 1869, and, like Döllinger, was revered in America and England as a champion of religious freedom.

8. The seventh mounted soldier cannot with certainty be identified as a specific saint. It is a portrait of Theodore Roosevelt, Sr. (d. 1878), father of President Theodore Roosevelt. In March 1874, Roosevelt Sr., a prosperous New York merchant, contributed five hundred dollars to the building fund of St. Paul's.

The Breck Mosaics

FACADE

The two sections of the facade mosaics—for the tympanum and for the corners of the west window—were designed in 1909 by American muralist George William Breck, working closely with the rector, Dr. Walter Lowrie (see pp. 52–54). The mosaics were the gift of Dr. Lowrie's close friend and former parishioner from Newport, Rhode Island, Daniel Fearing. Fearing gave them in memory of his wife, Henrietta Strong Fearing, who died in Rome on 16 April 1908.

In the corners of the west window are the symbols of the four Evangelists, each holding a book inscribed with his name. Going in a clockwise direction beginning at the upper right is the eagle of St. John, the winged ox of St. Luke, the seated lion of St. Mark, and the angel of St. Matthew. The Evangelists are framed by a stylized mosaic border of chains and of rondels containing various representations of the cross.

The tympanum mosaic shows St. Paul under house arrest in Rome, a subject chosen by Dr. Lowrie. It is an explicit analogue to the situation of the Episcopal Church in Catholic Rome before 1870. More important, however, Dr. Lowrie meant the subject to recall the strength through reconciliation that came to Christ's one church after the martyrdom of Saints Peter and Paul in Rome (see pp. 53–54). The Latin inscription on the tympanum is taken from St. Paul's message to the Philippians (1:18): DUM OMNI MODO SIVE PER OCCASI-ONEM SIVE PER VERITATEM CHRISTUS ANNUNTIETUR ET IN HOC GAUDEO SED ET GAUDEBO ("Only that in every way whether in pretence or in truth, Christ is proclaimed! and therein I rejoice, yea, and will rejoice.")

Like Dr. Nevin before him, Dr. Lowrie believed it possible that Paul's hired dwelling in Rome, where he was placed under house arrest, may have been a part of the house of Pudens, the site of the present-day church of Santa Pudenziana, a few streets away from St. Paul's on the via Urbana. The attentive guard, leaning towards St. Paul, is clearly on the road to conversion. He wears the uniform of the praetorian guard more for purposes of narrative identity than for historical accuracy (Dr. Lowrie noted that plainclothes were the customary dress for house police.) As for the scribe, Lowrie favored the possibility that this man might be Luke.

INTERIOR WEST WALL

These mosaics by George Breck were unveiled on Christmas Day, 1913. John Pierpont Morgan and William H. Herriman were the joint donors, with Morgan's son assuming the financial obligation after his father's death that same year.

The Creation of the World, the awakening of Adam in the Garden of Eden surrounded by the creatures of the peaceable kingdom, and the earth civilized by man, fill the upper zone. The four panels within the arches below tell the Christmas story, combining the coming of the shepherds to the manger with the Adoration of the Magi.

An ornamental border interspersed by the twelve signs of the zodiac frames the Creation. At the top, on either side of the central hand of God, are the words in Latin: *In the Beginning God Created the Heavens and the Earth.* On the left, above the waxing moon, a comet shoots through the heavens over Bethlehem. To the right, a brilliant sun fills the sky over Jerusalem, where a solitary cross marks the hill of Calvary outside the city walls. Within the city are the Constantinian churches of the Holy Sepulchre and the Ascension. The Church of the Nativity stands in the center of Bethlehem, represented as an early Syrian church, since the design of the original Constantinian basilica is unknown.

Over the four bays of *The Adoration of the Magi and Shepherds,* an inscription proclaims: GLORIA IN EXCELSIS DEO ET IN TERRA PAX. The Wise Men, who approach from the left, wear Phrygian caps and dress to emphasize that they are indeed *magi,* priests of Zoroaster, who have travelled vast distances to come to a stable in Bethlehem. Behind the shepherds on the right are the cypress trees and villa of a typical Tuscan scene.

The west wall is intended to be seen as an integral whole, combining the themes of the Creation of the World and the Redemption of Man through the Coming of Christ.

The Stained Glass Windows

The seventeen commemorative stained glass windows were already in place by the time of the consecration of the church on 25 March 1876. Designed and executed by the London firm of Clayton and Bell, they follow a specific plan of subject and treatment chosen by the first rector, Robert Jenkins Nevin. The three lancet windows, which were originally designed for and placed in the lower section of the apse, were removed in 1907 and imposed over the windows in the south clerestory. As part of the conservation work now in progress on the church it is planned to set them in a screen for the Canterbury Chapel to give them once again a visible location.

The three windows represent events in the life of Christ. Following the original placement, the Annunciation and Nativity (given in memory of Julia Augusta Stevens) are in the center; to the right is the vision of the risen Christ to St. Paul on the road to Damascus (given by the Right Reverend William Bacon Stevens, Bishop of Pennsylvania, in memory of the first bishop of that See, the Right Reverend William White); on the left is the taking of Christ by Roman soldiers and Pilate presenting Christ to the mob on Good Friday— "Ecce Homo" (given in memory of the Right Reverend Alonzo Potter, Bishop of Pennsylvania, who in 1859 became the first clergyman to hold an Episcopal service in Rome).

The eleven windows of the nave narrate events in the life of St. Paul as taken from the Acts of the Apostles. The windows are double-lights except for the single first window to the right of the main doors looking out. In the trefoil and quatrefoil lights above are representations of the Apostles and of St. John the Baptist.

NAVE WINDOWS

1. Upper: St. Paul as a youth, brought up by Gamaliel. Lower: scene with Nathaniel. The inscription reads ECCE VERE ISRAELITA. (Given in memory of the Rev. Somerset Burtchaell.)

2. Upper: Paul on the road to Damascus. Lower: the stoning of Stephen. Quatrefoil: St. Peter. (Given in memory of Desier Alstyne.)

3. Upper: laying on of hands, the ordination of Paul to the apostolate. Lower: the healing of Paul's blindness. Quatrefoil: St. Andrew. (Given in memory of James Brooks.)

4. Upper: Paul stoned and found by the Disciples. Lower: priest of Zeus bringing oxen for sacrifice. Quatrefoil: St. James Major. (Given in memory of George Risteau Amoss.)

5. Upper: dispute before the Apostles (?). Lower: Paul welcomed by the Apostles (?). Quatrefoil: St. John the Younger. (Given in memory of Cornelia Burrowes.)

6. Upper: Paul preaching to the Athenians. Lower: Paul beholds the Altar to the Unknown God. Quatrefoil: St. Phillip. (Given in memory of John W. and Mary Anne Smyth.)

7. Upper: running aground on Malta. Lower: Eutychus is returned to life by Paul. Quatrefoil: identification not clear. (Given in memory of Emily P. Wood.)

8. Upper: Paul receives women into the Church (?). Lower: Paul preaches to the heathen (?). Quatrefoil: St. Thomas. (Given in memory of American sculptor Thomas Crawford whose "Armed Freedom" stands at the apex of the capitol in Washington, D.C.)

9. Upper: a centurion delivers the prisoners to the guard in Rome. Lower: Paul and the viper on Malta.
Quatrefoil: identification not clear. (Given in memory of Hartmann Kuhn.)

10. Upper: Paul in prison writes to Timothy and is brought food. Lower: Paul appeals to Caesar. Quatrefoil: identification not clear. (Given in memory of John Alstyne.)

11. Upper: burial of St. Paul in the catacombs at Rome. Lower: Paul's martyrdom at the Tre Fontane in Rome. Quatrefoil: St. Jude. (Given in memory of the Right Reverend Samuel Seabury, D.D., Bishop of Connecticut, and first bishop of the Church in America.)

BAPTISTRY WINDOWS

12. Upper: St. Paul's own baptism. Lower: baptism of his household and jailer at Philippi. Quatrefoil: St. Simeon. (Given in memory of Mary Ludlum Cass.)

13. Upper: Christ gathering the little children to Him. Lower: Christ commands the Apostles to go and baptize all the

nations. Quatrefoil: John the Baptist. (Given in memory of Charles Marshall Haseltine.)

WEST WINDOW

14. The rose window in the west wall figures Christ in the center, his hand raised in blessing. In the smaller surrounding medallions are eight early Roman martyrs: Saints Ignatius, Agnes, Sebastian, Cecilia, Lawrence, Pudenziana, Clement, and Petronilla. The window was given in memory of Sigmund H. Horstman and his daughter Sallie H. Horstman.

An Itinerary of the Church

1. The wrought iron fence and garden wall cost $2,000 and were a gift of William H. Herriman. (Lowrie, *Fifty Years*: pp. 36 and 53). The ironwork was designed in 1875 by the church architect, George Edmund Street. The contract for the execution of the work was signed 28 July 1879 with the English firm of Thomas Potter and Sons. Two of the drawings are in the collection of the Royal Institute of British Architects. (Richardson: p. 122)

2. In the church garden are two small Roman cinerary urns in sarcophagus form, dating from the first or second century A.D. The two large sarcophagi date to the Severan period at the end of the second or beginning of the third century A.D. Dr. Lowrie mentions that two sarcophagi were the gifts of Dr. Nevin to St. Paul's, but he does not specify which ones. The rough stone vessels in the garden were found during the digging of the foundation. Three Roman oil jars were discovered on the site of the rectory, suggesting that this may have been the location of an early Roman oil shop. One of these jars was sent to Grace Church on Broadway in New York (the church that lent its name to the first Episcopal congregation in Rome). A second jar went to the Twombley villa at Newport, Rhode Island, home of one of St. Paul's most generous benefactors, Catherine Lorillard Wolfe. The third jar remains in St. Paul's garden by the entrance to the sacristy.

3. In the inner courtyard are several pieces of antique sculpture, including an important sarcophagus with lionhead decoration. The fountainhead was carved and given to St. Paul's in 1977 by sculptor Peter Rockwell.

4. The central entrance of the church faces via Nazionale.

The Great Doors for Christian Unity were dedicated on 28 April 1977 as a tribute to the ecumenical leadership and Christian charity rekindled by Pope John XXIII. The idea of memorial doors, open to the new spirit of *aggiornamento,* originated with the rector Dr. Woodhams, following Pope John's death in 1963. Dimitri Hadzi, a Roman resident for over twenty years and a parishioner of St. Paul's, volunteered to design and execute the doors. (Hadzi, who maintains an active studio in Rome, has been at the Carpenter Center for the Visual Arts at Harvard University since 1973, where he is Professor of Visual and Environmental Studies.) Incised on the door frames in Italian and English are the words of St. John, taken as a guide by John XXIII, "That all may be one." The left door leaf, which expresses the discord and instability of the divided churches, is a complex weaving of the instruments of punishment and suffering; by contrast, the right leaf appears open and harmonious, drawing together elements that symbolize unity through reconciliation. (For further background on the doors see pp. 73–75)

5. The baptistry is located in the first bay of the side aisle on the south; the walls of the baptistry support the campanile or bell tower. Around the inner wall, on a band of red marble from Perugia, runs the inscription: *The Rector, Wardens and Vestry in thankful memory of John David Wolfe first Trustee and constant friend of this church by whose daughter* [*Catherine Lorillard Wolfe*] *also this tower was erected to the glory of God.* The sheathing of the walls in *fior di pesca brecciata* was carried out by Dr. Lowrie shortly after he became rector.

6. The inscription at the base of the baptismal font, set in a base of marble called *giallo di Siena* reads: *To the Glory of God Amen and in loving memory of Emma Hyde wife of George W. Wurts of Philadelphia United States of America. Rome April 16 AD 1880.* The basin is of a white marble, probably from

Carrara, known as *calacata macchia d'oro*; it is supported by a pedestal of serpentine with columns of French red marble from the Pyrenees.

7. Two commemorative plaques, listing the names of donors to St. Paul's, are opposite each other. The one on the nave pier, of bronze inlaid with silver letters, records the names of the principal benefactors who contributed to the building and decoration of the church up to 1926; the marble plaque opposite, reflecting by its brevity diminished support of the church over the past fifty years, will continue to record benefactors as they come forward:

THE CHIEF BENEFACTORS OF S. PAUL'S

MDCCCLXXI—MDCCCCXXVI
Catherine Lorillard Wolfe

Mary Elizabeth Field	William H. Herriman
Martha Dod Stevens	Junius S. Morgan
William Waldorf Astor	J. Pierpont Morgan

Catherine Lorillard Spencer

Adeline Schermerhorn	Robert J. Nevin
George P. Clapp	Daniel B. Fearing
George W. Wurts	Hickson W. Field
Alice Nevin	Osgood Field
John Nevin Sayre	Francis Sayre
Elizabeth H. Woodward	A. D. Jessup
John C. Phillips	Mrs. Edson
Emily H. Hills	Laura Astor Dei
Mary J. Wyncoop	Edyth Feddi
Henry Chauncey	Wm. Bacon Stevens
Fanny H. Evans	Mrs. John P. Howard
John David Wolfe	Mrs. Griegg

Wm. Stanley Haseltine   Helen Marshall Haseltine
F. Auguste Schermerhorn   F. W. Stevens
Elizabeth W. Horstman   Mrs. G. M. Wilkins
John A. King   Jane Carter
Cornelia Ward   Julia A. Emmons
Baroness A. L. Des Granges   Emily J. Cowles

Ellen Schermerhorn Auchmuty

Harriette Foote Armour

Virginia Lowery Duchess De Arcos

John Gray   Janet Grover
Henrietta Tower Warts   Jessica Morgan
Adeline Gurd

BENEFACTORS OF ST. PAUL'S

MCMXXVII TO —

Adeline E. Gurd   Elizabeth Sampson Woodruff
Merrill McKay   Patricia and Thomas Tinsley
Ethel Richardson   Katherine Smoot Tuccimei
Patty Gurd Wilson   Carolyn W. Keene

8. On the first pier to the right on the south side of the nave is the Man of Sorrows, or *Ecce Homo*. A marble relief sculpture of uncertain date, it is believed to have come from Dr. Nevin's private collection.

9. The baptismal font at the head of the south aisle is medieval, again probably a part of Dr. Nevin's private collection. This is the font normally in use today, as baptisms are incorporated into the regular church service and witnessed by the congregation. The red granite column stub beside the font is used as a serving table.

10. The two ambones formed the ends of the choir rail as it was originally designed by the architect, George Edmund Street. It is likely that they were in place shortly after the consecration of the church in 1876. The pulpit is inscribed to *George W. Woodward, d. May 10, 1875,* the lectern to *Julia Rosa Newberry, d. in Rome April 10, 1876.*

11. The bronze peacock gates were dismounted and placed in frames in 1969 when the chancel was rearranged to accord with the new liturgy. The decorative motif is drawn from Christian iconography. Paired peacocks, with heads thrown back to behold the central cross, are surrounded by intertwined palmettes, oak leaves, vines, and grape clusters. The left gate is inscribed TE DEUM LAUDAMUS and, at the bottom, *In Memoriam Fanny Whitehead + March 11 1868*; the right gate, TE DOMINUM CONFITEMUR and *In Memoriam Caroline M. Gilfillan + July 2 1878.*

12. The memorial plaque above the sacristy door is to Robert Jenkins Nevin, first rector and principal builder of St. Paul's Within the Walls. The plaque was ordered by Dr. Nevin's successor, the Reverend Walter Lowrie, in 1907. The portrait of Nevin is a collaborative work of George W. Breck, painter and designer of the mosaics for the west end of St. Paul's, and the Italian sculptor named Granchelli. The inscription reads:

> *Born in Allegheny Pa. 1839. Died in Mexico City 1906. Buried at Arlington Va. Soldier for Union and Freedom in U.S. of America 1862–1868. Builder of this church of St. Paul in Rome where he came as Rector in 1869 and served faithfully till his death. This temple is his monument.*

13. The *piscina* and the *sedilia* with three seats were given in 1888 by Mrs. William H. Herriman. The surrounding decorative marble work, extending to frame the door of the

sacristy, was apparently paid for in 1907 by her husband, a vestryman and substantial benefactor of the church. This sequence of stonework and intarsia is notably fine work of the period. The designer is unknown.

14. The Bishop's Chair was given to St. Paul's largely by subscription from the English and Scottish Churches from which the American Episcopal Church derives its succession. It was first used during the consecration of St. Paul's, on 25 March 1876, by the Presiding Bishop in Charge of Foreign Churches, the Right Reverend A. N. Littlejohn, Bishop of Long Island. The chair was originally placed behind the altar, where the height of the retable visually decapitated the Bishop by blocking from view all of his body below the neck. The chair was moved to the north wall of the apse in the nineteen-thirties, shifted back to its original position in 1948, and given more visibility in 1969 when the altar was moved forward and the retable lowered.

15. The wooden altar, with a six-inch Carrara marble *mensa,* is a memorial to Dr. Nevin's brother, Richard Cecil Nevin, D.D. The altar was originally set forward from the wall in accordance with the traditional manner of a basilica, and preceded by a flight of three alternating red and white marble steps. In 1969 it was lowered a step and moved six feet forward. (For the reordering of the chancel, see pp. 67–71.)

16. The retable is inscribed on the back: *To the Glory of God Amen and in Loving Memory of Tillie Nagle Jessup + July 13, 1867.* The marble base was removed in 1969 to provide a better view of the Bishop's Chair.

17. The alabaster and mosaic decoration of the lower apse wall was the gift of Mrs. F. A. Delano, perhaps together with Mrs. A. D. Jessup, in 1881. (Lowrie, *Fifty Years:* p. 34) The eight large panels of alabaster have been worked in the

antique manner, presenting leaves of stone like *foglie* of a manuscript. Four slices of alabaster are arranged within each frame, with a profusion of patches, particularly in the centers, to enrich the natural patterning of the stone. The provenance of the seven alternate mosaic sections, as well as of the alabaster panels, is not clear. The Vestry notes of 4 April 1881 state that "the choice of the parties who should be entrusted with the mosaic work was made subject to the approval of the giver." The marble pieces form a design of ripening fruits, plants, and flowers within a checkerboard frame. The work is clearly related to Antique pavements and one strongly-held theory is that they are indeed Roman mosaics, beautifully preserved, and similar to pavements on the Palatine. The other argument suggests that they are exceptionally fine late-nineteenth-century workmanship in the Antique mode.

18. The Chapel of St. Augustine of Canterbury was dedicated in November 1976 (see pp. 62–63). Although several changes were made, the chapel retains the *cipollino* walls dating to the 1920s, and the following inscription: *In Loving Memory of Florence Lathrop Page and of Thomas Nelson Page, Ambassador to Italy 1913–1919 and Warden of this Church, this Chapel is Given by Their Daughters and Grandchildren.*

As preparation for the new dedication, a bronze and gilt tabernacle was designed for the altar by Elizabeth A. B. Jones, a professional medallist and parishioner of St. Paul's whose work includes portraits and commemorative medals for institutions and governments around the world. The four mosaic coats of arms were also designed by Elizabeth Jones for the chapel. Reading clockwise from upper right are the arms of Canterbury, the arms of York, the seal of the Episcopal Church, and the seal of the Anglican Consultative Council. The sanctuary lamp was given by Miss Carolyn

Keene in memory of her father, Francis B. Keene, American Consul General at Rome.

To make space for the new tabernacle the alter gradine of *fior di pesca* was split in the middle and the tabernacle placed between the two halves.

The notable stone cross is believed to have come from Dr. Nevin's collection. The style of carving and the simple decoration suggest that it is Roman, related to the church of San Clemente in Rome.

19. The two large glass and wood benches were designed as windbreaks after the church was built. They stood for many years inside the main entrance doors.

20. The wooden pulpit, formerly attached to the column at the head of the north aisle, was designed in 1909 by George Breck for Dr. Lowrie, who did not wish to preach from the north ambone. The pulpit was the gift of Daniel B. Fearing (who also gave the facade mosaics), and bears a memorial inscription to his wife, Henrietta Strong Fearing, who died in Rome on 16 April 1908. Dr. Lowrie chose as an inscription for the outside of the pulpit: *If ye know these things happy are ye if ye do them.* Sometime after 1926 he penciled his own graffito on the inside in bold letters, the words of Jacob: *How dreadful is this place.* The increasingly competitive rumbling of buses on via Nazionale has forced the introduction of an amplification system. In 1962 Dr. Woodhams returned to preach from the ambone and had the pulpit moved to its present position on the north aisle.

21. The terracotta *Pietà,* a gift to St. Paul's from the sculptor Edward Hoffman, was completed while Hoffman was artist-in-residence at Henry Clews' Chateau La Napoule outside of Nice.

22. The original oak entrance doors to the church have wrought iron decorative scrolls and hinges designed by the church architect, George Edmund Street. The doors were put on display inside the church when the new bronze doors were hung in 1977.

Appendix

Measurements of the Building

THE FOLLOWING dimensions of St. Paul's Within the Walls are taken from the measured drawings of architect Paolo Marconi, January 1977.

INTERNAL	METERS	FEET
Length east to west	39.64	130'
Depth of apse	5.5	18'
Width of nave between columns	8.7	28'6''
Width of nave to center of columns	9.51	31'2''
Width of apse	8.7	28'6''
Width of aisles, column face to wall	3.45	11'4''
Width of aisles to center of columns	3.78	12'5''
Baptistry	3.45 × 3.45	11'4'' × 11'4''
Circular tower stair, diameter	1.53	5'
Length of each of six bays, column center to column center	4.73	15'6''

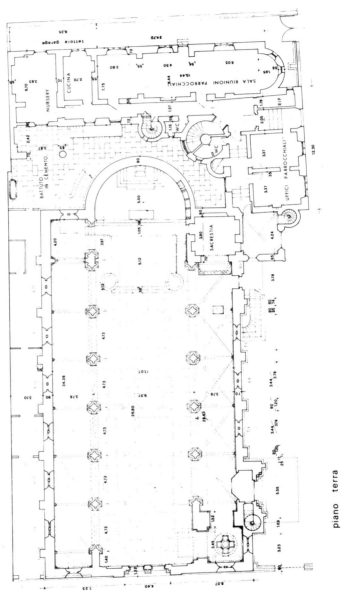

Plan and measurements of St. Paul's Within the Walls by
architect Paolo Marconi, January 1977, Rome.

EXTERNAL	METERS	FEET
Length east to west	42.75	140'
Width at front including tower	19.7	64'7''
Width through body of church outside	18.67	61'3''
Thickness of north walls	.95	3'
Thickness of south walls	.7	2'3''

HEIGHTS	METERS	FEET
Floor to roof inside	18.10	59'4''
Clerestory walls, from floor to top of cornice	15.40	50'6''
Aisle walls, exterior	7.45	24'3''
To apex of roof in front	19.7	64'7''
To top of tower, excluding ball and cross	42.40	138'9''
Clear height of Undercroft	3.1	10'2''

Contributing Artists to the Building Fund in 1871

THIS LIST of the nineteen original works of art donated to the Building Fund of St. Paul's Within the Walls by artists working in Rome is taken directly from the contemporary 1871 catalogue that accompanied the paintings and sculpture when they were taken to the United States for sale. (See pp. 24–26.)

View of Assisi — J. O'B. Inman
Venetian Fishing Boats — Mr. Tilton [sic]
Roman Contadine — Luther Terry
View on Seine near Paris — C. C. Coleman
View in Gardens of Villa Medici — D. Maitland Armstrong
View at Capri, Grand Marina — Wm. H. Haseltine
View on Lake Como — Prince George von Solms
Temple of Vesta, with House of Rienzi — Abby O. Williams

Peasant of the Roman Campagna — Mary E. Williams
View at Capri — Charles Temple Dix
Venice in the Distance — F. C. Welsch
Spring Effect Outside the Porta San Lorenzo — Wm. Graham

A Country Girl — George H. Yewell
Italian Buffaloes — C. Coleman
Ideal Head — E. Vedder
View near Rome — G. Inness
The Three Mary's at the Tomb* — T. Buchanan Read
Ideal Bust (sculpture) — W. H. Rinehart
Divine Wisdom (sculpture) — George Simmonds
Ideal Bust (sculpture) — H. Haseltine

* "This painting Mr. Read was not able to finish in time to send to the collection."

Rectors of St. Paul's Within the Walls

Robert Jenkins Nevin, D.D. 1869–1906

Walter Lowrie, D.D. 1907–1930

Theodore Sedgwick, D.D. 1930–1934

Samuel Tyler, D.D. 1934–1939

Appleton Grannis 1939–1940

Hiram Gruber Woolfe 1940

Hillis Latimer Duggins. 1946–1954

Charles A. Shreve. 1954–1957

Gerardus Beekman. 1958–1960

Wilbur Charles Woodhams. 1961–1981

Selected Bibliography

A REFERENCE to all the literature touching relevantly on St. Paul's Within the Walls would be too vast for the purposes of this history and guide. Richard Dorment's eight-page bibliography for his dissertation is certainly the most exhaustive survey of titles to date relating to the church, and particularly to the decoration through 1907. The few titles that follow have been of particular interest or use in preparing this history, and where they are cited in the text they are preceded by the abbreviations listed below.

"American Church of St. Paul, Rome." *The Architect,* XIV, 20 November 1875, p. 288.

ARMSTRONG:
Armstrong, David Maitland. *Day Before Yesterday.* (Edited by his daughter.) New York: Scribner, 1920.

Benedetti, Maria Teresa. "I Mosaici di Burne-Jones nella Chiesa di San Paolo entro le Mura a Roma." *Paragone d'Arte,* February 1978, pp. 40–60.

GB-J I OR II:
Burne-Jones, Georgiana. *Memorials of Edward Burne-Jones.* 2 vols. London: Macmillan and Co., Ltd., 1904.

"La Chiesa Episcopale Americana in Roma." *Illustrazione Italiana,* Anno III, No. 25, 16 April 1876.

Caffin, Charles H. "Mosaic in the American Church at Rome." *Harper's Weekly,* XLIII, No. 2194, 7 January 1899, pp. 9–10.

DORMENT, DECORATION:
Dorment, Richard. *Burne-Jones and the Decoration of St. Paul's American Church, Rome.* Ph.D. Dissertation. Columbia University, 1975.

DORMENT, ROMAN MOSAICS:
Dorment, Richard. "Burne-Jones's Roman Mosaics." *The Burlington Magazine,* CXX, No. 899, February 1978, pp. 73–82.

Howell, Peter. *Victorian Churches.* London, RIBA Drawing Series, 1968, pp. 34–35.

LOWRIE, FIFTY YEARS:
Lowrie, Walter. *Fifty Years of St. Paul's American Church, Rome.* Rome, 1926.

LOWRIE, PETER AND PAUL:
Lowrie, Walter. *Ss. Peter and Paul in Rome.* London: Oxford University Press, 1940.

LOWRIE, LITURGY:
Lowrie, Walter. *Action in the Liturgy.* New York: Philosophical Library, 1953.

Meeks, Carroll L. V. "Churches by Street on the via Nazionale and the via del Babuino." *The Art Quarterly,* XVI, No. 3, 1953, pp. 215–228.

Miles, Roy. "Viva Victoria." Catalogue of Summer Exhibition of 19th Century Paintings 4 June to 27 June 1980. London: 1980.

Millon, Henry A. "G. E. Street and the Church of St. Paul's in Rome." *Essays in Honor of Henry-Russell Hitchcock,* in press.

THE BUILDER:

"Modern Work in Rome." *The Builder,* XL, No. 1991, 2 April 1881, pp. 383–394.

NEVIN:

Nevin, Rev. R. J. *St. Paul's Within the Walls: An Account of the American Chapel at Rome, Italy.* New York: D. Appleton and Co., 1878.

RICHARDSON:

Richardson, Margaret, ed. *Catalogue of the Drawings Collection of the Royal Institute of British Architects,* Vol. S, Farnborough, 1976.

"St. Paul's American Church, Rome." Rome: DAPCO, 1959.

STREET, A. E.:

Street, A. E. *Memoir of George Edmund Street, R.A., 1824–1881.* London: John Murray, 1888.

Street, George Edmund. *Brick and Marble in the Middle Ages: Notes of A Tour in the North of Italy.* London: John Murray, 1855.

TANI:

Tani. A. D. *New Guide to Rome.* Rome: Enrico Verdesi, 1925.

VESTRY MINUTES:

St. Paul's Parish Archive. The Vestry Minutes are entered in sequential ledgers.

Index

Page numbers of the black and white illustrations are set in italics.

INDEX

Fearing, Henrietta Strong (Mrs. Daniel B.), 88, 101
Feddi, Edyth, 96
Fedeli, Emily Nancrede, 66
Feilden, Bernard, 72
Fence, garden, 36, *37*, 94
Field, Hickson W., 79, 96
Field, Mary Eleanor, 79
Field, Mary Elizabeth (Mrs. Hickson), 44, 79
Field, Osgood, 96
First Vatican Council, 13–14
Fisher, Most Rev. Geoffrey, 70
Foundations, 28–29
Francis, Saint, 82
Franco-Prussian War, 19
Friends of the American Chapel in Rome, 26

Gabriel, 80–81, *Fig. 3*
Gamaliel, 91
Garfield, James A. (Pres.), 87
Garibaldi, Giuseppe, *84*, 87
Genesis, 80
George, Saint, of England, 83, *84*, 87
Gilfillan, Caroline M., 98
Giovanni XXIII, *see* John XXIII (Pope)
Glass windbreaks, 101
Grace Church (New York), 94
Grace Church (Rome), 13, 21, 23
Graham, William, 106
Granchelli (sculptor), 51, 98
Grannis, Appleton (Rect.), 67, 107
Grant, Ulysses S. (Pres.), *84*, 87
Gray, John, 97
Great Law Courts, London, 27
Gregory I (Pope), Saint, *84*, 85
Gregory Nazianus, Saint, *84*, 85
Griegg, Mrs. 96
Grover, Janet, 97
Gubbio, 66
Gurd, Adeline E., 66, 97

Hadzi, Dimitri, 31, 74–75, 95, *Fig. 9*
Hancock, Thomas, 47
Hancock, Winfield Scott, *84*, 87

Harvard University, Carpenter Center, 95
Haseltine, Charles Marshall, 93
Haseltine, H., 106
Haseltine, Helen Marshall, 97
Haseltine, Wm. Stanley, 97
Herriman, Mrs. William H., 51, 98
Herriman, William H., *84*; as donor, 36, 51, 55, 85, 89, 94, 96, 99
Hills, Emily H., 96
Hoffman, Edward, 101
Holland, Thomas J. B., *37*
Horner, Frances, 39
Horstman, Elizabeth W., 97
Horstman, Sallie H., 93
Horstman, Sigmund H., 93
Howard, Mrs. John P., 96
Howell, Peter, 36
Hyacinthe, Père (Charles Loyson), *84*, 87

Ignatius, Saint, 93
Illustrazione Italiana, L', 35
Independence Hall, Philadelphia, 19
Inman, John O'Brien, 24, 106
Inness, George, 24, 26, 106
International Center for Preservation and Restoration of Cultural Property, Rome, 72

James Major, Saint, 91
James of Spain, Saint, 83, *84*, 87
Jerome, Saint, *84*, 86
Jerusalem 55; Church of the Ascension, 89; Church of the Holy Sepulchre, 89
Jessup, Mrs. A. D., 99
Jessup, Tillie Nagle, 99
John the Baptist, 91, 93
John, Saint, 80, 88, 95
John Chrysostom, Saint, *84*, 85
John the Younger, Saint, 91
John XXIII (Pope), 15, 19, 63, 73–75, 95
Jones, Elizabeth A. B.: mosaic shields, *61*, 62, 100; tabernacle, *61*, 62, 101
Jude, Saint, 92

113

This book was set in Bembo type
by the DEKR Corporation, Woburn, Mass.,
printed on Finch Opaque paper at
the Transcript Printing Co., Peterborough, N.H.,
and bound at the Northeast Bindery, Portland, Maine.
Designed by W. L. Bauhan